CULTURES OF THE WORLD

BRUNEI

Tamra B. Orr

Marshall Cavendish
Benchmark

New York

PICTURE CREDITS

Cover photo: © Robert Harding Picture Library Ltd/Alamy

alt.TYPE/Reuters: 33, 38, 92, 108, 109 • Art Directors & Trip: 5, 44, 68, 122, 123 • Attar Maher/Corbis Sygma: 70, 106 • Benhamou/Prestige/Getty Images: 32 • Bettmann/Corbis: 98 • Bob Krist/Corbis: 121 • Carol Wiley/ Lonely Planet Images: 10, 18 • Charles & Josette Lenars/Corbis: 56 • Chris Heller/Corbis: 22 • Christopher Furlong/Getty Images: 14, 49 • Dean Conger/Corbis: 76 • Dean Conger/National Geographic/Getty Images: 21, 69 • Francis Tan JY: 130, 135 • Getty Images: 15 • Holger Leue/ Lonely Planet Images: 40, 63 • Holger Leue/Getty Images: 127 • Ira Block/ Getty Images: 118 • Jeremy Horner/Corbis: 80, 90 • Louise Lister/ Getty Images: 125 • Michael Nicholson/Corbis: 28 • Michael S. Yamashita/Corbis: 73 • Paul Chesley/Getty Images: 79 • Peter Anderson/ Getty Images: 13 • photolibrary.com: 1, 3, 4, 6, 7, 8, 9, 11, 12, 16, 17, 20, 23, 24, 30, 39, 46, 48, 51, 53, 54, 55, 57, 58, 59, 60, 62, 64, 66, 67, 74, 81, 84, 85, 95, 97, 99, 101, 103, 104, 105, 111, 119, 126, 128, 129, 131 • Richard I'Anson/ Lonely Planet Images: 19, 34, 78 • Roslan Rahman/AFP/Getty Images: 42, 94, 114, 115, 117 • STR/AFP/Getty Images: 37 • Todd Gipstein/ Getty Images: 124 • Wayne Walton/ Lonely Planet Images: 82

Preceding page
A group of Bruneian schoolgirls.

Publisher (U.S.): Michelle Bisson
Editors: Christine Florie, Stephanie Pee
Designer: Benson Tan
Copyreader: Kristen Azzara
Cover picture researcher: Connie Gardner
Picture researcher: Thomas Khoo

Marshall Cavendish Benchmark
99 White Plains Road
Tarrytown, NY 10591
Web site: www.marshallcavendish.us

Originated and designed by Times Media Private Limited
An imprint of Marshall Cavendish International (Asia) Private Limited
A member of Times Publishing Limited

All Internet sites were correct and accurate at the time of printing. All monetary figures in this publication are in U.S. dollars.

Library of Congress Cataloging-in-Publication Data
Orr, Tamra B.
  Brunei / by Tamra B. Orr
    p. cm. (Cultures of the world)
  Includes bibliographical references and index.
  Summary: "Provides comprehensive information on the geography, history, governmental structure, economy, cultural diversity, peoples, religion, and culture of Brunei."—Provided by publisher.
    ISBN 978-0-7614-3121-3
1. Brunei Islands—Juvenile literature. I. Title.

DS650.3.O77 2009
959.55—dc22   2007047043

Printed in China
7 6 5 4 3 2 1

CONTENTS

A Bruneian girl.

A wide variety of wildlife can be found in the forests of Brunei.

INTRODUCTION

ALONG THE COAST OF THE South China Sea lies the tiny country of Negara Brunei Darussalam, or Brunei for short. The country did not achieve independence from Britain until 1984. The peoples' lives are guided by Islamic principles and the philosophy of Melayu Islam Beraja, a blending of Malay cultural customs and Islamic law and values.

Thanks to the discovery of oil, Brunei is a wealthy place. However, as reserves begin to dwindle, the nation has had to look in new directions to support its economy. With virtually no natural disasters, little pollution, and even less crime, Brunei continues to be just what its name implies—an "abode of peace."

GEOGRAPHY

TUCKED IN THE UPPER EDGE of the Malaysian state of Sarawak is the country of Brunei. Slightly smaller than Delaware, at 2,226 square miles (5,765 sq km), it is easy to miss when you first glance at the island of Borneo, since it is just a tiny part of the third largest island in the world. Brunei is surrounded by the Malaysian state of Sarawak, except for its northern side that is bordered by the South China Sea. In fact, part of Sarawak sticks up right to the coastline, splitting Brunei into two pieces.

Brunei's culture, history, and language are all heavily influenced by its close proximity to Singapore, Malaysia, and the southern Philippines. The cultures share many similarities but have a few important differences as well.

Most of Brunei is built on a bedrock of shale, sandstone, and clay. The western portion of the country has a few small hills, while the eastern

Left: **An aerial view of the Omar Ali Saifuddin Mosque and Brunei's capital city of Bandar Seri Begawan.**

Opposite: **Brunei is home to beautiful and lush rain forests such as the Ulu Tamburong National Park.**

side has flat coastal plains that slowly turn into Brunei's few mountains. The west and northeast regions of Brunei have a number of swamps lined with mangrove trees. In the north is 161 miles (259 km) of coastline made up of white, sandy beaches. The color comes from silica, a mineral which is commonly used to create such items as glass and concrete.

Brunei is home to four major rivers. The smallest is the Temburong, while the Belait is the largest, covering 1,052 square miles (2,700 sq km). At one end it courses through jungles, while at the other, swampy forests. The mouth of the river is often full of sandbars.

The Tutong River wanders through 502 square miles (1,300 sq km) of the Tutong Basin. It is full of sand pits and sandbars, and near its upper part is Tasek Merimbun, Brunei's largest lake. The Brunei River flows through tropical jungles, the Port of Muara, and urban areas.

The numerous plant and animal varieties found in Brunei are also found in neighboring Malaysia, which is considered to be one of the world's megadiverse areas, with more than 14,000 species of plants and trees, 600 species of birds, 210 species of mammals, and thousands of species of insects.

FROM FORESTS TO FRONDS AND FRUIT

An incredible three-quarters of Brunei is covered in forest. Taking timber out of the forests to sell is banned by law; logs can only be used for local purposes. In areas where trees are cut down, new ones are planted immediately. Forest conservation is very important to the people. They want to preserve what they have and keep it beautiful. They also want to keep their forests healthy and fertile, because it brings ecotourists, or visitors interested in learning more about the environment, to the region. This works to support their economy. In some areas there are dense rain forests overflowing with life; in other areas there are mangrove swamps or heath forests. All of them are considered by experts to be among the richest and most diverse ecosystems in today's world. The *apong* or nipa tree is found there as well. It is a tall tree with palm tree-like leaves or fronds, which when dried are used to construct the roof or walls of a house. The long stems of the fronds are used to make fishing poles, while sap from the flowering portion is made into sweet syrup. The tree grows a nutty-tasting fruit whose seeds are edible and used in a number of local recipes.

The rain forests of Brunei explode with different species, from palms and shrubs to bamboo and herbs. In one spot moss grows, while in another creepers hanging from tree limbs. The pitcher plant's pouchlike tips are actually death traps for any curious insects that stop by to have a sip of dew.

Above: **The benign looking pitcher plant is actually a carnivorous plant that traps insects for food.**

Opposite: **Brunei's Belait River.**

The mangroves of Brunei are some of the best in all of Southeast Asia. Thick and hardy, these trees are home to many different plants and animals. Shrimp and other fish raise their young among mangrove roots, and migrating birds stop by for easy snacks. In the past the mangroves were important to the people of Brunei because they provided everything from food and medicine to building materials.

Inside the mangrove forests are a number of exotic plants. The *jeruju*, or sea holly bush, has prickly leaves that were thought to ward off evil spirits and were placed in bundles under a house when a woman was in labor. Juice from its leaves was thought to make the hair shinier and healthier, and the roots and seeds were used to make creams for treating conditions like boils or nasty coughs. The small, bushy *anggeriting*, or Lumnizera tree, is easy to spot in the forest because of its bright red flowers. Its wood is extremely hard and is sometimes used for bridges, flooring, and even tool handles.

LONG NOSES TO STRIPED FINS

Primates of many different kinds live in the forests of Southeast Asia. The orangutan population has declined over the years, and now these apes are primarily found on just a few islands.

THE QUEEN OF PARASITES

One of Brunei and Malaysia's most famous plants is the huge rafflesia. Known as the queen of parasites, it is certainly an unusual plant—but not one anyone would want in a garden.

First, it is huge, often reaching 3 feet (1 m) or more in diameter. Second, it is covered in white spots that look a lot like giant warts. Third, this plant has no clear leaves, roots, or stems. Fourth, and definitely worst of all, unlike most flowers, it has a horrible smell. In 1928 the entomologist E. G. Mjöerg stated that it had "a penetrating smell more repulsive than any buffalo carcass in an advanced stage of decomposition." In the past the flowers of the plant were ground up and used to help stop excessive bleeding after childbirth. Today the plant is used for an entirely different purpose: to fascinate tourists. As this plant becomes rarer, a number of people from around the world, especially ecotourists, are eager to come to Brunei and Malaysia to see it.

Gibbons, with their small, thin bodies, short legs, and long arms, spend most of their lives up in the trees, swinging from one place to another. The loud, harsh hooting sound they make is one of the most distinctive noises heard in this region. Leaf-eating monkeys known as langurs like to climb but spend a lot of time on the ground as well.

One type of monkey found almost exclusively in Brunei is the proboscis. In Malaysia, proboscis monkeys are threatened, but in Brunei there are approximately 10,000 of them living in the forests and mangrove swamps. They have large, long noses and big bellies. Their tails are long and pale, and their fur is orange brown. They do not come to the ground often but have been known to go swimming. Proboscis monkeys are most active at dawn and in the late afternoon, when the sun begins to set.

At dark approaches, another interesting Brunei resident comes out: the giant mudskipper. This odd character spends as much time in the water as it does out of it. Although it is considered a fish, at least half of its waking hours are spent on land. It has eyes on the top of its head and is known to get aggravated if another mudskipper comes along and tries to move in on its territory, especially if it is breeding. These creatures are carnivorous and eagerly search out a meal of insects, snails, or ever smaller mudskippers. True to their name, some species of mudskipper are able to walk, jump, and skim across both water and land.

Other animals found in this region include the catlike civet; the tapir, which looks like a cross between a wild pig and a hippopotamus; and the pangolin, or scaly anteater. More than 100 types of bats fly overhead in search of insect dinners. One of the main food sources for these bats is biting midges, or sand flies. They are tiny, usually between 0.06 and 0.16 inches (1.5 and 4 mm), but great numbers of females are known to attack anything tasty—including people! At dusk and dawn, the midges are known for swarming around people's faces, scalp, and hands.

Left: **The curious look-ing Malayan tapir is the largest of four species of tapirs.**

Opposite: **The endangered proboscis monkey thrive in the forests and swamps of Brunei.**

With the South China Sea nearby, there are many different marine creatures in Brunei. One of the most interesting, however, is the *ikan pelaga* Brunei, or the Brunei beauty. For more than 50 years this fish was thought to be extinct, but it was rediscovered in 1981 in one of Brunei's waterfalls.

The Brunei beauty is about 4 inches long (10 cm). The male has a colorful body and typically has red and black stripes on its front fin. The most noticeable thing about the fish, however, is its large mouth.

WARM AND WET

The people of Brunei are used to the hot and humid weather of their country. Temperatures tend to stay between 76 and 86 degrees Fahrenheit (24–30° C) all year round. Though there is no set rainy, or monsoon, season,

A man shelters himself from the rain in Kampung Ayer. The people of Brunei are accustomed to heavy rainfall all year round.

Brunei is often very wet. It averages 110 inches (2,800 mm) of rain per year on the coast, and up to 150 inches (3,810 mm) per year inland.

Unlike some of the surrounding countries, which have suffered greatly from devastating earthquakes, tsunamis, and massive flooding, Brunei almost never suffers from natural disasters.

EXPLORING THE DISTRICTS

Brunei is divided into four main districts, three of which are in the much larger western section of the country. Each district has a capital and other cities, as well as *mukims*, or provinces.

The largest district is the westernmost one, Belait. It is at the heart of the nation's economy, as it is the center of oil and gas production. Belait is home to about 70,000 people and covers almost half of the country. The main town is Kuala Belait, which contains an odd combination of a traditional Malay village called Kuala Balai and homes for many of the foreign workers, including the Dutch and Filipinos brought in to work in the oil and gas industry. One of the district's cities, Seria, was little more than a swamp called Padang Berawa, or Wild Pigeon's Field, before oil was discovered. An oil prospector who explored the area in 1926 said, "Walking here means really climbing and jumping over naked roots and struggling and cutting through air roots of mangroves of more than a man's height." Today, against the sunset's silhouette, are rows of "nodding donkeys," or oil pumps bringing up gallons of black gold from the ground.

Rows of oil drills dot the landscape of Brunei.

The district to the east of Belait is Tutong. This is Brunei's agricultural zone, where a variety of crops are grown, from coffee and tapioca to cinnamon. Fewer than 35,000 people live there, many of them fruit and vegetable vendors who sell their products at the huge Tamu Tutong, or produce market. At the Rumah Budaya cultural village, visitors can get a glimpse of Brunei's different ethnic groups and their lifestyles.

Brunei's largest lake is found in this district. The Tasek Merimbun snakes back and forth over 19,274 acres (7,800 ha). In 1984 it was declared a National Heritage Site by the Association of Southeast Asian Nations (ASEAN).

The next district over, straddling the northern bank, is Brunei-Muara. Although it is the smallest of the four districts, it is home to 180,000

Brunei's largest lake, Tasek Merimbun, was declared a World Heritage Site in 1984.

people, which is half of Brunei's population. The capital of Brunei, Bandar Seri Begawan, locally known as BSB, is located there. Until 1970 it was simply known as Brunei Town. This city is Brunei's seat of power, as it is where the sultan and his family live most of the time and the center of Brunei's foreign businesses, finance, and government. It is a fascinating combination of modern office buildings and huge mosques and features some of the nation's most beloved and well known landmarks.

LIFE IN KAMPONG AYER

One of the most unusual towns is Brunei-Muara's Kampong Ayer, or water village. Approximately 30,000 people live there in a maze of houses,

The city of Bandar Seri Begawan.

mosques, and schools, with wooden promenades or decks connecting them to each other. Each building is supported by a set of sturdy stilts, and has been for centuries. When the explorer Antonio Pigafetta visited the area in 1521, he described the city as "entirely built on foundations in the salt water . . . it contains twenty-five thousand fires or families. The houses are all of wood, placed on great piles to raise them high up." Later, he christened it the "Venice of the East." Water taxis escort the people from place to place. Along with the homes are medical clinics, mosques, fire and police stations, and shops.

The fourth district is the far eastern Temburong. It has been physically cut off from the rest of Brunei since 1890. This part of Brunei is much

Children along one of the walkways that connect the houses of Kampong Ayer.

A DAY IN THE WATER VILLAGE

In this excerpt from Eric Hansen's "The Water Village of Brunei," the experience of what it must be like to live in such an unusual place is described:

In the gathering purple-blue light, this village of about 30,000 people appeared as several enormous clusters of houses on stilts, all moored in tight formation in the middle of a bend in the Brunei River. As the village slowly wakened, the clattering footsteps of children and commuters along Kampong Ayer's rickety wooden walkways, known as *jembatan*, were joined by the growing bass rumble of motorized *tambangs*, or water taxis, as they ferried people to the nearby shore. There, buses and cars waited to take them to work throughout Bandar Seri Begawan, the capital city of Brunei that today virtually surrounds Kampong Ayer.

Soon after the morning commute subsided, women began to drape the wooden balconies of the village with lines of freshly washed batik sarongs and children's clothes. Bedding was aired, and, as the sun reached the household balconies, woven mats were set out and spread with prawns, small fish and *krupuk*, the distinctive dried-prawn crackers of Southeast Asian cuisine. Every additional bit of balcony space seemed to overflow with cascades of orchids and bougainvillea. Beneath the houses, open boats bobbed in the river. Little boys lowered crab pots from bedroom windows. Telephones rang, cats and lizards took up sunny positions on the wooden walkways, and the sounds of hammers, saws, and boiling teakettles indicated that another day was in full swing in Kampong Ayer.

less developed and has a sparse population of Malay, Iban, and Murut peoples. Much of the district is made up of rain forests, and the Ulu Temburong National Park is located there. It stretches across 193 square miles (500 sq km). It features a scientific research lab and a rain forest studies center. The main town in this district is Bangar, the only actual town in the whole area. It can only be reached by boats, which are referred to as flying coffins because of their shape.

The Ulu Temburong National Park is located in the far eastern region of Temburong.

To visit this district is to see the Brunei of long ago. The jungles are untouched. Cultural groups live as they have for countless years. More evidence of this can be seen in the nearby Amo C, a five door Iban longhouse in which tourists are allowed to stay for a few days to experience this traditional lifestyle.

Despite Brunei's size, it has an amazing amount of diversity. It is a country that has been independent only for a little more than 20 years, but has hundreds of years of history and culture.

The interior of an Iban longhouse.

HISTORY

BEFORE BRUNEI EXISTED AS a nation, it was simply another part of Southeast Asia, as was Malaysia and Singapore. Humans have lived in the region for thousands of years, and as more excavations are done, more is learned about the people who once lived there.

IN THE DISTANT PAST

One of the earliest indications that people were living in the archipelago was found in 1958 in the Niah Cave of peninsular Malaysia. A skull found there dates back approximately 40,000 years. In 1991 a complete skeleton was found in a Malaysian cave called Gua Gunung Runtuh in the Lenggong Valley. It is more than 10,000 years old, making it from the Paleolithic era, also known as the Stone Age. Based on the way he was buried—curled in the fetal position and surrounded by stone

Left: **Evidence that humans were living on the archipelago was found in the Niah Cave.**

Opposite: **The burial jars of high-ranking individuals in some ethnic groups in the region were housed in elaborate structures, such as this burial pole, which is known as Klirieng. These poles are often made out of ironwood and have detailed carvings on them.**

tools—experts believe that he was an important man in his community. A few years later an 8,000 year-old-skeleton of a woman was found in a nearby cave.

The earliest signs of human presence in this area come from Malaysia's Bukit Jawa. Archaeological finds there date back 200,000 years. Another important site is located in the Kota Tampan area in Ulu Perak. Digging began there in 1933, and an incredible 50,000 pieces of stone tools have been found and catalogued. Experts believe this site was inhabited approximately 74,000 years ago.

The first people thought to have come to Brunei were the Orang Asli from southern China, and the Negritos, from eastern and western Malaysia. Many of these people originally came from southern Indochina.

The Orang Aslis are considered to be one of the first inhabitants of Brunei.

They were followed by the Senoi in roughly 2500 B.C. This group brought better stone tool- and pottery-making skills with them. The Proto-Malay filtered in from the Indonesian islands from about 1500 to 500 B.C. They initially lived on the coast and then slowly began moving inland.

TIME FOR TRADE

By the first century A.D. the area had become an important shipping port. People living there traded often with India and China. The jungles of the area produced aromatic and durable woods, resins, and bird's nests, while nipa palms provided thatch for roofs and walls. These items were sold to merchants or traded for cloth, pottery, and glass. Chinese traders were also attracted to the area by the tin being mined, as they used it in sculptures. The Chinese also obtained pearls and tortoise shells for making jewelry, and sea slugs, which they used in a variety of medicinal preparations.

Some of the merchants who came to Brunei's shores during the second century were searching for something even more valuable: gold. Stories told by travelers hinted that Brunei, Singapore, and Malaysia were rich in gold, earning them the name Aurea Cheronese, or Peninsula of Gold. Although these Chinese and Indian traders did not find any gold, they had a strong impact on the Malay people and their culture through their introduction of new beliefs, such as Hinduism and Buddhism.

By the beginning of the seventh century the Malay had noticed that many of the ships passing through their waters frequently had to stop for several months to wait for the winds to change. To take advantage of these sailors while they were waiting, the Malay created entrepôts, or storage ports. They built settlements along the shore so that they could

A bust of Afonso de Albuquerque, who led the Portuguese in attacking Melaka.

that went very wrong. Although the Portuguese traders were welcomed at first, upon the advice of his Muslim counselors, the sultan ordered an attack on the ships, taking 19 prisoners in the process. Now it was time for the Portuguese to take revenge. This time they came prepared, with 18 armed ships. In less than a month's time the Portuguese had defeated the empire and taken control. They would remain in control for 130 years but were not well liked, especially because they kept trying to spread Christianity.

Portugal's control was challenged by the Spanish. Ferdinand Magellan came to Brunei's shores in 1521 on his voyage around the world. In 1529 the two settled their land dispute through the Treaty of Zaragossa, which gave Spain the Philippines, while Portugal retained the Spice Islands, Malaysia, and Brunei.

The sultan of Melaka and his court fled the area, some to the north and some to the south. Those in the north set up an empire named Perak, while those to the south established Johor. For the entire time the Portuguese held Melaka, the Johor Empire never stopped trying to regain control.

THE JOHOR EMPIRE

At the end of the 16th century the Dutch came to the Johor Empire. Unlike the Portuguese who came before them, the Dutch were there to become allies with the empire and in turn make a fortune by taking control of the bustling spice trade. With the support of the Johor, the Dutch were able to take control of Melaka in 1641. The battle lasted for several months, but the Portuguese were thrown out of Melaka and the Johor took over leadership of the empire. To thank the Johor Empire, the Dutch lifted all taxes and trade restrictions that they had forced on the other states. By the end of the 17th century Johor was one of the strongest Asian powers in the region.

A VISIT TO BRUNEI

On Magellan's ship was a young geographer named Antonio Pigafetta, who wrote of their reception in this new land in Magellan's Voyage:

> When we arrived at the city [Melaka], we remained about two hours in the ship until two elephants covered with silk came, and twelve men, each with a porcelain jar covered with silk, to carry our gifts. Then we mounted the elephants and the twelve men marched ahead with the jars and gifts. . . . Then we went to the king's palace on the said elephants, with the gifts ahead, as on the previous day. Between the house and the king's palace all the streets were full of people with swords, spears and targets, for the king had willed it thus. . . .
>
> Then one of the chief men told us that we could not speak to the king but that if we desired anything we should tell him, and he would . . . speak through a speaking tube by a hole in the wall to the one who was inside with the king . . . we told him that we were servants of the King of Spain, who desired peace with him and required no more than to do trade. The king caused us to be told that since the King of Spain was his friend, he was very willing to be his, and he ordered that we should be allowed to take water and wood and merchandise at our will.

Sir James Brooke demanded that he be made the governor of Sarawak, in exchange for helping Brunei to quell civil unrest.

GAINING INDEPENDENCE

Johor was under the rule of Sultan Mahmud at the end of the 17th century. He was not a strong leader, and in an attempt to bring more money into the court, many people turned back to the old tradition of piracy, which scared off traders. Continual battles with a nearby Sumatran kingdom also made life more difficult. Finally, the people revolted and murdered the sultan.

During the mid-18th century, the Dutch continued to weave their cultures and traditions into the Melaka Empire. They rebuilt the areas that had been destroyed during the battle for control. Their grand ideas for development, however, were not as successful as they had planned. The Dutch administrators were living on limited salaries and found that much more money could be earned through the black market and taking kickbacks from grateful merchants. While this put more money in their pockets, it also damaged their reputation and trade declined.

In 1795 the Dutch were still in control but it was on shaky ground. Their defeat in the 4th Anglo-Dutch War had stolen their morale. They were not making the money they had hoped and it was clear that the British trading skills were superior to theirs. Finally, when the British made their move to take control, the Dutch did not protest.

In 1839 the face of Brunei changed with the arrival of the English adventurer James Brooke. He came to the region to help Sultan Omar Ali

Saifuddin II stop a civil war and gain control of Sarawak, the southern province of the sultanate. In return for his help, he demanded that he be made governor of Sarawak, which became recognized as a independent state in the 1850s. Under his rule, Brunei became smaller and smaller as Brooke and other White Rajahs, or British rulers, took increasing amounts of land, finally increasing Sarawak's size until it split Brunei in two. As more and more areas came under Britain's control, Brunei eventually became one of its protectorates in 1888.

During the mid-1800s many workers from China trickled into the area in search of work and a better life. By the middle of the century the Chinese made up more than half of Singapore's population, spilling over into other coastal towns on the west coast. They brought much of their heritage with them, forming *kongsis*, or clan houses, and triads, or secret societies. Often they came into conflict with the local Malays, resulting in a number of civil wars. Britain sent in officials known as residents who worked as civil servants to help support the sultan and settle problems.

As Britain's control continued to grow, it looked as if the reign of the sultan, one that had lasted for generations, was about to fail. By 1906 the area was controlled by a British resident, and the sultan had very little power. In 1929, however, oil was discovered, turning Brunei into an economic power virtually overnight. The sultan immediately arranged for all the money earned from oil to remain in Brunei, rather than being spread out throughout the rest of Malaysia. He did this by ensuring that Brunei did not unite with the other Malaysian states but instead remained a British protectorate.

Despite being under Britain's protection, Brunei was occupied by the Japanese during World War II until 1945. For four years the people of

Brunei endured bombing and occupation by the Japanese. When the war was over, the region had a lot of rebuilding to do.

In 1959 Sultan Omar Ali Saifuddin III announced Brunei's first written constitution. It stated that Islam was to be the state religion and that Britain would continue to be in charge of the country's defense and foreign affairs. Three years later Britain pushed Brunei to hold elections for the first time. The Brunei People's Party wanted to keep Brunei independent and remove the sultan from power. When it won all ten elected seats on the council, however, the sultan grew angry. He declared a state of emergency, allowing him to stay in power. The following year, in 1963, Brunei made the decision to stay independent rather than join Sabah, Sarawak, and Singapore in the creation of the Federation of Malaysia.

Sultan Hassanal Bolkiah became the sultan after his father, Sultan Omar Ali Saifuddin abdicated the throne.

In 1967 Sultan Omar Ali Saifuddin abdicated and his son, Hassanal Bolkiah, became the sultan. He is still leading the country today. He is the 29th ruler of his line, and it was through his efforts that Brunei achieved independence from the British in 1984.

In the last two decades Brunei has been one of the richest nations in the world. It is also one whose culture centers on Islam. In 1990 the sultan introduced the national ideology of Malay Islamic Monarchy, or Melayu Islam Beraja, which attempts to blend Malay tradition with Islamic values. The next year, in accordance with Islamic principles, alcohol was banned, and a stricter dress code was put into place. In 1992 the sultan made the study of Islam mandatory in all schools.

Toward the end of the 20th century Brunei's royal family has had to deal with some scandal, as the sultan's younger brother had to be removed from the court for overspending. This puts Sultan Bolkiah's eldest son, Prince Al-Muhtadee Billah, as the next in line for sultan of Brunei. In 2004 the sultan agreed to reopen parliament 20 years after it had been disbanded. Although this was seen as a positive step, the sultan amended the constitution to allow only 15 of the 21 members to be elected rather than appointed.

The crown prince of Brunei, Haji Al-Muhatdee Billah.

GOVERNMENT

THE PEOPLE OF BRUNEI ARE proud of the fact that their country has one of the oldest reigning monarchies in the world. Their current sultan is the 29th in a line of rulers reaching back more than 600 years.

Opposite: **A government building on Jl Elizabeth Dua Street.**

The first ruler was Sultan Muhammad Shah, also known as Awang Alak Betatar. It was he who originally spread Islam among the Bruneians. The fifth ruler in line was Sultan Bolkiah, and it was under his strong and determined leadership that Brunei expanded into an empire, with territories reaching into parts of the Philippines and out across Borneo. During the reign of the ninth ruler, Sultan Hassan, Brunei's royal court experienced such luxury and splendor that it was the envy of most surrounding empires.

The 22nd sultan, Muhammad Alam, was known as the King of Fire. He was a vicious warlord, rumored to be a cannibal and apparently so cruel that even his own sister tried to kill him. When he finally recognized that he was not well liked by the people, he was given the choice of either surrendering or be killed. He chose death and was publicly garroted, or strangled.

Brunei was ruled by sultans all the way through its becoming a British protectorate, an area under Britain's protection. Even after British residents came to Brunei, the sultan maintained his position. Over the first quarter of the 20th century the sultan began to lose power as the country was granted internal self-government. However, with the discovery of oil in 1929, things began to change. Although Sultan Omar Ali Saifuddin III helped Brunei create a new constitution in 1959, he did so reluctantly. The constitution has been amended twice, in 1971 and 1984.

In 1967 Brunei's current sultan, Haji Hassanal Bolkiah Mu'izzaddin Waddaulah became the 29th ruler of Brunei. During his rule Brunei gained independence, and its people adopted the philosophy of the Malay Muslim Monarchy, referred to as MIB (Melayu Islam Beraja).

A NATIONAL PHILOSOPHY

Melayu Islam Beraja is fairly new to Brunei, but the idea goes back centuries. The concept of political Islam spread to the Malay area some time after the 13th century, but it took until the 14th century for Islam to become Brunei's official religion. On January 1, 1984, Sultan Hassanal Bolkiah officially announced that MIB was to be the nation's "guiding light" for the Bruneian way of life. By accepting this philosophy, the nation agreed to observe holy days in the Islamic calendar and to make prayer a part of government functions and projects. Brunei's government site states that

> The nation hopes through the true adoption and practice of the MIB philosophy, the purity of Islam, the purity of the Malay race and the institution Monarchy can be maintained and preserved as a lasting legacy for future generations.

The Chinese who live in Brunei are conflicted about this idea of having a state religion. Most Chinese are not Islamic and the MIB excludes them, making them feel like second-class citizens.

LIFE AS A SULTAN

Brunei is officially an independent sovereign sultanate. The sultan is the head of state, with full authority. To support and advise him are five councils: the Religious Council, which helps the sultan with issues or questions dealing with the Islamic faith; the Privy Council, which advises the sultan on constitutional matters and on giving out royal pardons and royal titles; the Council of Succession, which determines the succession to the throne; and the Council of Cabinet Ministers and the Legislative Council. The Legislative Council is supposed to keep a close eye on legislation in Brunei, but it has not met for years, thanks to a royal

THE 29TH LEADER

His Majesty Sultan Haji Hassanal Bolkiah Mu'izzaddin Waddaulah (*below right*) became crown prince in 1961. On October 5, 1967, he became sultan after his father, Al-Marhum Sultan Haji Omar Ali Saifuddin Sa'adul Khairi Waddien, abdicated the throne.

Sultan Bolkiah was born on July 15, 1946, in Brunei's capital. He studied in institutions in both Brunei and Malaya and then went to the United Kingdom to receive additional education. He entered the Sandhurst Royal Military Academy and was promoted to captain in 1967. He had to leave in the same year to take on his role as sultan. In addition to being Brunei's leader, he is also the prime minister, defense minister, finance minister, and head of religion. The sultan does a great deal of traveling throughout Southeast Asia, East Asia, the Middle East, Europe, and the United States.

In addition to his governmental work, the sultan also enjoys playing polo and is husband to Her Majesty Raja Isteri Pengiran Anak Hajah Saleha and father of four princes and six princesses.

THE NATIONAL FLAG

Brunei's flag is divided into four parts. In the middle is the state crest. The background of the flag is yellow, white, and black. It is red in the center, and on the crest it says "Always in Service by God's Guidance" in Arabic. The crest includes a *sayap*, or wing with four feathers, which stands for justice, tranquility, prosperity, and peace; a *tangan*, or hand, which represents the government's pledge for peace, and a *bulan*, or crescent, which is a symbol of Islam. Under the crest it says "Brunei Darussalam," or Brunei, the Abode of Peace.

proclamation made against it in 1984. In 2004 the sultan brought back the idea of electing people to government positions rather than appointing them, but so far, that free election has not taken place.

The next person in line for the throne is the sultan's oldest son, Prince Haji Al-Muhtadee Billah. Born on February 17, 1974, he is His Majesty's third child. For much of his life he has focused on studying Islamic teachings. While waiting to take over the leadership of his country, the prince has been involved in many government agencies so as to learn more about how Brunei works.

The sultan and everyone in his family lead luxurious lives. Istana Nurul Iman, the royal palace, is the largest palace in the world. It is located in Brunei's capital city. Built in the 1980s, it contains 1,788 rooms and somewhere between 3,000 and 5,000 cars. Hundreds of these cars are Rolls Royces, complete with bulletproof glass, leather interiors, huge television screens, and satellite navigation systems. Newspaper reports say that the palace contains more than 250 toilets, 51,000 lightbulbs, 18 elevators, and 44 staircases. The sultan's four thrones are lit up by a dozen 1-ton chandeliers and sit in front of an arch tiled in 22-carat gold. The palace is the perfect place to hold a party, as the banquet halls seats 4,000, and the prayer hall seats 1,500. Visitors who happen to fly in by helicopter can land on the helipad on the roof. In addition to this huge palace, the sultan also has homes in London, Paris, Los Angeles, and New York.

The sultan's royal chamber.

Recent expenses for the sultan have included $2.5 million for his badminton coach and another $2.5 million for his acupuncturist and massage therapist. He paid more than $100,000 to the guards of his exotic birds. Currently, he owns 5,000 vehicles, 2 jets, 6 small planes, and 2 helicopters. The sultan is listed as one of the richest men in the world, with an estimated net worth of more than $22 billion.

As extravagant as the sultan's lifestyle is, he recently had to deal with someone who spent money even faster and more casually than he did: his younger brother, Prince Jefri. In his role as finance minister, Prince Jefri spent money so quickly and excessively that the sultan removed him from the position in 1997. One example of Prince Jefri's ultraexpensive projects is the six-star Empire Hotel. It includes everything from a golf

A suite in the Empire Hotel, one of the world's most luxurious hotels.

course and multiple restaurants to a bowling alley, movie theater, three swimming pools, and its own beach. It has 360 rooms, plus dozens of villas and suites. Reports state that it cost more than $1 billion to build, involving thousands of craftspeople from several nations. The atrium in the middle of the hotel is 82 feet (25 m) high, with marble columns and walls covered with gold Islamic designs. The lobby staircase is decorated with 370 tiger's eye gemstones, and the railing is covered in mother-of-pearl and other semiprecious stones.

Prince Jefri did not spend tremendous amounts of money just on building hotels; he also spent it on himself. He bought five luxury hotels overseas, 2,000 cars, several jets, and homes so lavish that they included gold-plated toilet brushes. In fact, by the time he was caught, Prince Jefri had spent more than $4 billion on personal expenses. When he was finally relieved of his position in the government, the sultan gave him a budget of $300,000 a month to live on, but Prince Jefri just kept spending. He did have four wives and 35 children to support. Finally, the sultan had had enough. The allowance stopped, and men were sent after the prince to get back some of the $16 billion missing from government coffers.

GETTING TO KNOW YOU

At the end of the holy month of Ramadan is a celebration known as Hari Raya. For the Muslims of Brunei, it is a festival that focuses on asking forgiveness of others and on strengthening close relationships. For three days the sultan opens his palace to the public. He also allows locals and tourists to stand in line in order to meet him and other members of the royal family. It is a long wait. In 2007 more than 95,000 people stood in line for this opportunity to meet the sultan.

The prince's belongings were auctioned off. Unexpectedly, in 2006 the sultan agreed to drop charges against his brother and pay the legal costs involved in tracking him down. At last report, however, the brothers are not on speaking terms.

THE BRUNEIAN MILITARY

The military in Brunei is made up of the Royal Brunei Armed Forces, which includes an army, a small navy, and an air force. All of it is made up of volunteers. Because of Brunei's close ties with Britain, the military is supplemented by the British Armed Forces Gurkha battalion and the

Sultan Hassanal Bolkiah inspects the troops during Brunei's National Day celebrations.

Royal Brunei Malay Reserve Regiment. The role of the armed forces in Brunei is fourfold. The armed forces are to do the following things.

1. Deter any external powers that attempt to undermine, either directly or indirectly, the integrity of Brunei and to stop any subversive elements operating inside Brunei.

2. Undertake military operations to counter aggression, terrorism, or insurgency.

3. Assist in maintenance or public order in support of the police and civil authority, if called upon.

4. Maintain good community relations so that the armed forces can be identified with the government and the nation's population.

THE NATIONAL ANTHEM

Brunei's national anthem is dedicated to the sultan. Just after the end of World War II a group of young Bruneians decided that Brunei should have its own anthem, as other countries did. Awang Haji Besar bin Sagap wrote the music, while Pengiran Haji Mohamed Yusuf bin Abdul Rahim wrote the lyrics. Like most songs, the anthem went through several revisions and finally was introduced to schoolchildren in a Malay school in Pekan Brunei. Titled "Ya Allah langutkanlah Usia" or "God Bless His Highness," here are the lyrics:

God bless His Majesty
With a long life
Justly and nobly rule the Kingdom
And lead our people happily forever
Peacefully be, the Kingdom and Sultan
Lord, save Brunei, the Abode of Peace

ECONOMY

UNLIKE MANY SMALL COUNTRIES IN the world, Brunei has had very few concerns about poverty. With a low unemployment rate and a high standard of living, it has remained one of the wealthiest nations on the planet. Almost all of its economy is based on oil, however, and since supplies will eventually run out, the government has been looking in new directions for sources of money. It is just in time, too. There have been concerns voiced about how the country's money has been spent and what that might indicate for the near future.

Opposite: **An oil well at Seria. The discovery of oil has made Brunei one of the wealthiest countries in the world.**

DOWN IN THE MINES

The discovery of oil in 1929 transformed this little country from unknown to well known. Before oil was found, coal was one of the most important products in its growing economy. Coal was in great demand in the 19th century; it was needed for fuel for steamships, trains, and other engines. When coal was found on the island of Labuan, off Borneo's coast, in 1844, the British interest in it was one of the forces that propelled Britain to annex the island from Brunei.

Most of the coal mining took place in Muara, the westernmost district of Brunei. Between 1889 and 1924 the Sarawak government operated the mines, bringing up tons of coal. At first the miners used nothing more than hoes, shovels, and hammers, but as time passed, more sophisticated and powerful equipment was brought in to speed things up. All of this activity turned Muara from a small town into a bustling city, with shops and a growing population. Just after Muara was returned to Brunei, in 1921, the price of coal began to drop. Soon the mining became less profitable and was stopped. It was brought back temporarily during World War II, but only for long enough to provide fuel for the local people.

ON THE RUBBER PLANTATIONS

Another temporary source of income came from rubber plantations. Rubber had become an important commodity when automobiles began using rubber tires. By the turn of the century the region was establishing estates to grow it. Soon the area became the world's largest producer of natural rubber. In order to run these plantations, the British landowners brought in Indians from Tamil and Nadu.

Rubber is produced by first cutting a shallow culvert, or gash, into the bark of a rubber tree. A milky white substance known as latex then runs out. It is collected in a cup, and a few days later, the whole process is repeated.

The latex is taken to a processing center, where it is smoked over a fire and shaped into large, solid sheets. From there it is made into everything from rubber globes to car tires. Once oil was found, rubber plantations began to fall by the wayside, and most have now disappeared.

The rubber plantations continued to do well into the 1950s. Brunei's second largest plantation crop, oil palm, also began to take hold in the country. Palm oil is made from the fruit of the oil palm. This product was first introduced to the region in the 1860s, and by 1917 the first

Opposite: **The sap of the rubber tree, or latex, is collected in small cups before being sent for processing.**

palm oil plantation was established. Although the tree is native to Africa, seeds were brought over from Sri Lanka, and they did extremely well in the Bruneian climate.

The oil palm tree produces a very large fruit that is packed with oil. Picking and harvesting the fruit is a tricky and risky job. It involves climbing up a high ladder and reaching in amid the stiff, sharp palm fronds to pick the fruit. Most of the danger, however, lies on the ground, because the underbrush in oil palm plantations is the perfect place for poisonous snakes to live. After the fruit is picked, the rind and the kernels are separated. While the oil comes from the rind, the kernels, when crushed, also creates an oil that is used in such products as margarine or cooking oil. In recent years, as people around the world have become more health

A LOOK AT LIFE ON THE PLANTATION

In John S. Major's book *The Land and People of Malaysia and Brunei*, he describes life on a rubber plantation in the past. He writes

> Six days a week, he gets up at five in the morning to be able to start work at dawn, going out in a truck with other workers to the section of the estate, that the foreman has decided to tap that day. He cuts a new groove in the bark of each tree, and makes sure that the coconut-shell cup in its wire holder is placed so that no latex will seep past it. After cutting bark until late morning, he and his fellow workers eat their noon meal among the trees and rest before going back to retrace their steps from the morning, emptying each cup into a large metal pail. At the end of the day, each worker's pail is weighed. . . . After the pails are weighed and recorded, each worker empties the pail into a vat in the back of a truck, and the day's work is ended.

conscious, the demand for this high-saturated-fat oil has decreased. These plantations, like the rubber ones, have faded away in Brunei.

FINDING BLACK GOLD

The first oil well in Brunei was dug in 1899, near present-day Bandar Seri Begawan. Oil had been seeping up to the surface, a good clue that more would be found down below. Six oil companies were eager to determine the size of the reserve. When the find turned out to be small, most of those companies pulled out of the region. It was not until 1929 that the first productive oil well was dug, at Seria in Belait. Seria was little more than a swamp then, full of dark red water not fit for human consumption. By 1932 oil was being exported to other lands, and the sultan was able

An oil refinery in Seria.

A MONUMENT TO OIL

Next to the Seria oil field, rising up like a spider with long black legs, is the Billionth Barrel Monument. Commissioned by Brunei Shell Petroleum and designed by a Bruneian, it was built in 1991 to honor the production of the billionth barrel of oil from this location. The former managing director George Innes said, "The celebration today is to mark the coming of age of the Seria Field which has produced one billion barrels of oil and deservedly merits its place in the ranks of the world's giant oil fields. This has not been solely achieved by technological advances but also by consistent human endeavor over the past six decades."

to pay off all the country's debts. Virtually overnight, Brunei went from a small, unrecognized country to an economic power. Many historians believe that if oil had not been found, Brunei would never have even tried to become an independent country.

Even though bombing sustained during World War II tore up many of their oil fields, the fields kept producing, averaging 15,000 to 19,000 barrels each day. The Brunei Shell Petroleum Company kept drilling exploratory wells until 1960. After that, they began drilling offshore. In 1963 the first offshore oil field was discovered, just off Kuala Belait, and was commissioned in 1972. Soon the Brunei Liquefied Natural Gas plant was in full operation. Between 1969 and 1979 four large oil fields were found, and production went up to 250,000 barrels a day.

The money that has come from Brunei's more than 300 oil wells exceeded the expectations of investors as well as of the people of Brunei. In 1953 the sultan decreed that Brunei would become a welfare state and that he would spend thousands of dollars to make sure that each citizen was given free health care, a free education, and social security for those too old or unable to work. In addition, houses and cars are often partially paid for by the government and if a Muslim wants to make a pilgrimage to Mecca, the holy land in the Islamic faith, the government will help pay for it. Brunei does not impose an income tax.

BRUNEI'S CURRENCY

Brunei's coins come in 1-, 5-, 10-, 20-, and 50-cent denominations. Its bills are called Brunei dollars. Its bills come in increments of 1, 5, 10, 50, 100, 500, 1,000, and 10,000 dollars. Each one is colorful, decorated with a number of images of the sultan and his family, as well as familiar holy sites within the country.

IMPORTS AND EXPORTS

While Brunei exports an amazing amount of crude oil, petroleum products, and liquefied natural gas to Japan, the United States, and numerous Asian countries, it has to import almost everything else it needs. Agriculture and fishing supply some of the people's needs, but on a very small scale.

Rice is one of the most commonly eaten foods in Brunei, and most of it has to be imported, something the government is trying hard to change. In 1978 the Agriculture and Public Works Departments launched a large-scale rice-planting project in Kampong Wasan. Covering 988 acres (400 ha), it has helped to provide a portion of the people's food supplies. Any local planters who want to start their own paddy fields are supported by the government's Department of Agriculture. This support includes everything from easily available bank loans to access to equipment and technology.

A farmer tending to his rice field. Cultivating their own crops has helped Brunei to reduce its dependency on other countries for food.

Some fruit is grown locally and supplies about 11 percent of what the population demands. The Agriculture Department has also helped support fruit cultivation and has planted seeds to supply local favorites, such as rambutan, durian, and oranges. Vegetable growing has been more successful, fulfilling about 65 percent of the country's needs. Approximately 1,000 head of cattle and buffalo are raised in Brunei. Once again, the government helps farmers by paying for machinery, feed, seeds, fertilizer, and veterinary care. The rest of the meat needed by the people is imported from Australia.

LOOKING IN NEW DIRECTIONS

While Brunei has not had to worry about money for decades, the government recognizes that its oil and gas reserves will eventually run out. It also is aware that the money it has made in the past has not been spent wisely or cautiously. In 2000 the Brunei government announced that the time of financial excess might be coming to an end soon. "There are warning signals of fundamental economic problems which threaten to undermine the prosperity and with it the social stability enjoyed by the people of Brunei," said a government release. It went on to warn that continued prosperity "can no longer be taken for granted." It went on to state that "Unless government finance is strengthened, His Majesty's Government will be increasingly diminished in its ability to provide security, social services and infrastructure development." As one Bruneian stated, "You can't just wish away a lifetime of hand-out mentality and wastage."

Today, there are efforts to diversify the economy into finance and foreign investment, as well as ecotourism. The head of tourism Sheikh Jamaluddin bin Sheikh Mohamed hopes to promote Brunei as a "premium ultimate eco-tourism destination, unpolluted, safe, friendly and a good place to relax . . . a mystical place, rich in culture and tradition." He recognizes that because Brunei is a very small place, it cannot possibly support thousands of tourists. It does not have the public transportation systems, communication systems, or hotels. Instead, the government hopes to bring in a few ecotourists who want to spend their time enjoying the many beautiful natural sites in the country.

Brunei's vast fortunes have been made through oil and gas for more almost 80 years. Within two or three decades, however, supplies will run out, and the country will have to find other ways to generate income. Whether this income comes from foreign investment, business, tourism, or a combination of all three, it will alter the economy in ways that will lead Brunei in new directions.

Brunei hopes to capitalize on its natural beauty to boost ecotourism in a bid to diversify its economy.

ENVIRONMENT

ALTHOUGH BRUNEI IS fortunate that it is not beset by natural disasters and is amazingly free of air and water pollution, it still has important environmental issues to address.

The Bruneian government takes the environment and its protection seriously. Currently, more than 33 species are considered protected in Brunei, 11 of which are endangered, including the black-faced spoonbill and the Siamese crocodile. The white head and chest of the white-bellied sea eagle has been seen less and less frequently, and the badak sumbu, one of the smallest rhinoceroses in the world, is also endangered. The green turtle and painted batagur turtle are both endangered, and the stork-billed kingfisher, a bird with a large red beak, is disappearing. Current law states that anyone caught exporting any of the country's protected animals can be sent to prison for a year or be charged a $2,000 fine.

Left: **The white-bellied sea eagle is protected in Brunei.**

Opposite: **A waterfall at Brunei's Labi Recreational Park.**

PROTECTING THE RAIN FORESTS

In 2007 Brunei, along with Indonesia and Malaysia, signed a historic declaration called the Heart of Borneo. It states that all three countries will work together to protect and preserve their rain forests. "It has become clear since we started to discuss cooperation on the vision for the Heart of Borneo that the world outside our countries is excited by what we are doing and is prepared to lend us support," said Pehin Dr. Awang Haji Ahmad bin Haji Jumat, Brunei's minister of Industry and Primary Resources.

Brunei recognizes that educating young people about the environment is an important part of protecting it. At a recent tree-planting ceremony

Logging in Brunei. Brunei is determined to protect and preserve her rain forests.

WELCOME TO THE PARK

One of the best places from which to appreciate the diversity and beauty of Brunei's environment is the Ulu Temburong National Park, in Temburong. This 193-square-mile (500 sq km) park is so large it takes up one-tenth of the whole country.

People get to the park by taking an hour-long ride on a longboat through thick jungle. The park was set up not only for people to enjoy but also as a place in which to catalog the biodiversity of the Brunei rain forest. So far 170 species of ferns, 700 species of trees, and hundreds of thousands of species of insects have been identified.

Once inside the park one of its biggest attractions is the canopy walkway. To get to it, you have to climb across two precarious hanging bridges and over a plank way, and then climb stairs that are almost vertical as they curl around a 197-foot (60 m) aluminum structure. It is a lot of work, but it is more than worth it once you get to the top. From there you can see all the way to Brunei Bay in the north and to Gunung Mulu National Park in the south. Looking closer, you can see gibbons playing, squirrels running through the trees, flying lizards soaring from one tree to the next, and all colors of birds flying among the green leaves. To extend your visit to the park, you can charter a longboat to take you upstream to where a primitive tree house awaits. For the brave of heart the park staff also offers visitors night walks through the rain forest canopy.

in Tutong, Awang Haji bin Saidin Salleh, the director of Forestry, stated, "It [is] part of the department's ongoing awareness programmes involving schoolchildren to heighten their appreciation and understanding of the value of protecting the natural environment and its resources." The director emphasized the importance of the community's involvement in following forestry laws and regulations. In Brunei it is a violation for people to go into protected forest areas without prior permission from the forestry department. It is also an offense to take forest products without the proper permits. Those caught doing so face penalties that include fines and imprisonment. "Therefore, it is hoped that the public is always aware of the regulations and laws in force pertaining to forestry," said the director.

An olive ridley sea turtle. Three out of seven of the world's sea turtle species nest on Brunei's shores.

PROTECTING THE TURTLES

Of the seven sea turtle species found in the world, three of them come to the shores of Brunei to lay their eggs. Every year the green turtle, the hawksbill, and the olive ridley come up on shore. Recently, some of these species are becoming rare. To protect them, Brunei has launched the Turtle Conservation Programme, making it an offense punishable by a fine or even jail time for anyone to steal or sell turtle eggs.

Why do people take the eggs? Many Bruneians like to eat them. "These people ought to have reported their findings [of reduced numbers of nests] to the relevant authorities and helped conserve an endangered species,

Olive ridley turtle eggs, like other turtle eggs, are highly prized because many Bruneians like to eat them.

Littering is a serious problem in Brunei.

instead of taking the eggs home and eating them," said one turtle lover in Brunei. "It is frustrating to see things like this happen, especially when we try so hard to educate people about the dangers of extinction."

Other people drive their vehicles over the sand, crushing the eggs in the nests and scaring away the adult turtles with the noise and bright lights. Many people hope to get laws passed that bar cars from the beaches.

PROTECTING THE BEACHES

Another environmental problem that has been increasing within Brunei is littering, especially on the beaches. To help combat that, some organizations sponsor annual beach cleanups. When one was sponsored by the Girl Guides Association, Datin Hjh Jusnani Hj Lawie, vice president of the group, said, "With the planning of this campaign, the Girl Guides Association hopes to create an impetus which will encourage others to maintain the cleanliness of their surroundings. Maintaining a clean environment should be ongoing and not limited for the duration of the campaign only."

PROTECTING THE ENVIRONMENT

In 2000 the Environment Unit of the Ministry of Development initiated a number of important environmental projects, most of which the public cooperated with. However, one project did not get the response it hoped for from the people. The project's aim was to discourage the use of plastic bags, primarily in shops. Because they are made out of a nonbiodegradable material, they can do a lot of harm to the environment. One person in Brunei who is in favor of this project said, "In Brunei, people have been using the plastic bags in most of their daily activities. But we should remember in the old days people traditionally used the woven baskets and bags to carry their goods. Therefore I strongly believe that [banning the use of plastic bags] should not be a problem for the locals." He added, "Education is vital in this context and perhaps it should begin in schools and offices as well as public areas."

The concept of recycling is slowly taking hold in Brunei. Some schools are providing different bins for glass, cans, paper, and plastic. The government hopes that eventually, the practice will make its way into people's homes as well. A quick look at the landfill in Sungai Akar is often enough to remind the people of its importance. In 2005 a survey about waste management was taken. It showed that Brunei generated about 189,000 tons of waste per year, an average of 3.1 pounds (1.4 kg) per person per day. In 2007 the Minister of Development asked the public to focus on reducing the amount of waste being created. The new emphasis is on Reduce, Reuse, and Recycle. The ministers estimates that if people would do this, it would reduce the total amount of waste going into the landfills by 88 percent.

WORLD ENVIROMENT DAY

Brunei took part in the 2007 celebration of World Environment Day. The theme of the celebration was "Melting Ice—A Hot Topic," and it concentrated on how climate change affects polar ecosystems. The sultanate held a "Green Month" to emphasize the importance of recycling and taking other steps to protect the environment.

BRUNEIANS

DESPITE BRUNEI'S SMALL SIZE, it has a population of 374,577. The majority are Malay, but there is also a mix of Chinese, Indian, and a number of indigenous groups, which are some of Borneo's early inhabitants.

THE MALAY

Malays make up almost 67 percent of the population. However, exactly what defines a person as Malay is less than clear. At one time the definition was someone who was Muslim, spoke the Malay language, and had ancestors who came from the Malay Peninsula. The definition began to blur over time, however. Today, an easier term to use is *bumiputra*, or "son of the soil." This group is made up of Indonesians, Negritos, and Papuans, most of who originally came from central and western Sumatra.

Left: **Malays make up the majority of the population of Brunei.**

Opposite: **A young Malay boy from Kampong Ayer.**

Today, most of the Malays live in the cities and near the coast. Originally, most of them were rice farmers, but in modern times most have moved into jobs in the oil industry and the government. The majority of Malays can trace their ancestors to the royal family, as the sultan and his relatives are considered Malay.

THE CHINESE

The second largest ethnic group in Brunei is the Chinese. They constitute approximately 15 percent of the population, or 60,000 people. The Chinese originally came to the area in the 1800s as "coolies," people brought in by the British to work as laborers in the coal mines or on rubber, spice, or oil palm plantations. Their ancestors come from a variety of provinces in southern China. The number of Chinese in the

A Chinese woman buys produce at the market. After the Malays, the Chinese make up the next largest ethnic group in Brunei.

country increased immensely after the discovery of oil. Between 1931 and 1947 the Chinese population tripled, and it would be almost 40 years before the population growth began to slow.

Today, many Chinese are professionals, technicians, and store owners. They have been economically successful. Because of this, the Malay occasionally regard them with suspicion and jealousy. Chinese communities are scattered throughout Brunei, differentiated mainly by which part of China the people originally came from. The Quemoy Hokkiens, for example, are found primarily in Brunei-Muara, while the Hakkas, Cantonese, and Hainanese live primarily in Belait. Although there are many Chinese in Brunei, only 23 percent of them are actually Bruneian citizens. This is not because they do not want to be; it is because the rules for obtaining citizenship in Brunei are quite complicated. A detailed knowledge of Brunei's history and language is required. Other strict rules are also in place that make some suspect their very purpose is to discourage foreigners from trying to become citizens. Many of the Brunei Chinese have left to live in Australia or Canada.

ASIAN INDIANS

About 6,000 people living in Brunei are Asian Indians, and most of them are Hindu. The majority of them work in the service sector, especially in hotels and business industries. The country has also attracted immigrants from other Asian nations such as Taiwan, Pakistan, Nepal, Sri Lanka, Bangladesh, and the Philippines.

INDIGENOUS GROUPS

There are number of indigenous, non-Muslim groups living in Brunei, all of which tend to be labeled as Dayak. The largest subgroup within the Dayak is the Kendayans. In the past the Kendayan were rice farmers who worked directly for the sultan. Today they are culturally closer to the Malay, as a result of extensive intermarriage. The other, smaller groups are Bisaya, Penan, Murut, and Iban. Together, they made up about 15,000 people. While the Bisaya, Murut, and Penan have worked to blend in with the rest of the Malay, the Iban have concentrated on maintaining their distinct culture and continue to live in traditional longhouses virtually all of them working hard to make their living cultivating rice.

The interior of a long-house in Brunei.

THE SEA DAYAKS

The Iban are also known as Sea Dayaks. They are thought of as river and forest people who traveled from place to place in long canoes. The Iban once had a fearsome reputation as headhunters, as well as pirates. Today, almost all of them are rice farmers.

LIFESTYLE

ONE GLANCE AT THE STREETS of Brunei is enough for anyone to tell that it is an Islamic country. Besides the silhouette of the sultan's palace and the mosque against the capital city's skyline, the appearance of many of the people makes it clear. Their clothing and demeanor speak of their religion in multiple ways.

When two men of the Islamic faith shake hands, for example, they do it lightly and quickly, often just touching before putting their hands to their chests. If a man and woman meet, they do not touch at all, as it is not allowed. When Muslims point, they use their thumbs, with their fingers curled under. Women do not expose their knees or arms in public at any time, and shoes are always removed before entering a mosque or other sacred place.

Left: **Bruneian muslims on their way to the mosque for afternoon prayer. Islam influences all aspects of Bruneian life.**

Opposite: **A man carefully steps off a water taxi in Kampong Ayer.**

THE TURBAN TRADITION

One of the most significant symbols of the religion is the wearing of a turban. An Islamic prayer says "Allahumma salli'ala sahibi al-taj," which means "Our Lord, bless the Owner of the Crown!" In this case the crown is interpreted to be a turban. The length of cloth wrapped around the head involves two pieces of headdress. One is the *qalansuwa*, a borderless hat. The second is the *imama*, the actual piece of cloth that is wound around the hat. Wearing the two together is essential; wearing just one is considered offensive.

Ideally, the turban is made of white muslin, a type of cotton. The colors and length of the fabric varies. The typical length is between 7 and 10 yards (6.4 to 9 m). Many Bruneians wear this type of headgear when they are not wearing the locally traditional *kopiah*.

THE KOPIAH

During the month of Ramadan, Muslims buy new clothes in preparation for the celebration at the end of the month. They often purchase new wardrobes from top to bottom, including the turban option—the *kopiah* or *songkok*, as it is called in Brunei.

A *kopiah* looks a little like an oval hat with no brim, similar to a fez. Wearing one has been a tradition in Brunei for a very long time. At one time they were used to indicate a person's class or social status. Today, both men and women wear them as it is a symbol of being a Bruneian.

Over the years a number of modifications have been made to the *kopiah*. Pieces of paper or cardboard are sewn between the layers of fabric to make the hat stronger and more durable. The hats are custom made according to the specific shape, height, and head size of the person who is going to wear it. Most are black, although some other colors are available. *Kopiahs* known as *bergunung* have raised sides. *Kopiahs* known as *berlis* are covered in lace. Holes for ventilation are added to the top of the hat, since wearing one can get quite hot during the day. Some *kopiahs* have no stiffeners sewn into them, so they can be folded up or flattened.

Before adopting the *kopiah*, Bruneian males traditionally wore a different kind of head covering known as a *dastar* or *tanjak*. It is a traditional Malay head cover made out of thick fabric that is folded into a kerchief. The knot that holds the kerchief together is made so that it moves up to the top and curls slightly sideways as the *dastar* is tied around the head. Today, the *dastar* is normally worn by the groom during his wedding or by nobility during formal or special celebrations.

Many of Brunei's women wear a special kind of head scarf called a *hijab* whenever they are in public. It covers their hair and neck, according with Muslim religious practices. Since the acceptance of Islam, the popularity of head covers had more than tripled, because one of the tenets of the religion to keep something on the head.

Opposite: **A Bruneian man wears a turban while he sits with his wife, reading.**

OTHER STYLES

Although many of the Chinese wear western-style clothing, some stick to more traditional clothing. They wear loose outfits that are similar to American-style pajamas. While some young women might want to wear short skirts, this is offensive to Muslims and is considered an insult to their culture.

Some of the Indians living in Brunei choose to wear traditional clothing. Men occasionally wear a dhoti, a wrapped white skirt typically worn with a shirt or with a white tunic. Women wear a sari, a long, flowing silk or cotton wrapped dress over a short, tight-fitting shirt.

GOING TO SCHOOL

In Brunei education is free, and six years of elementary and up to seven years of secondary school is required. This is a relatively new rule. A mere century ago the literacy rate in Brunei was low. Today, it is almost 93 percent, one of the highest in the world.

In 1906 Brunei's education system underwent a huge change because Britain entered the picture. The British colonists wanted to introduce the western education model to the country but had to wait five years until teachers could be trained and the budget had enough in it to create the schools. Finally, in 1912 the first school was created. It was a Malay school in BSB. At first it operated from inside a mosque but then moved to a building previously used by the government. The first class consisted of 30 young boys. By 1915 the number had increased to 40. The Muara District opened its own school, and other districts followed over the next three years. The government got involved, and in 1918 it began sending students to the Teacher's Training College in Melaka.

Despite receiving support from the government, there were a number of families who did not want to send their children to these schools. Most students came from the upper class, and none of them were girls. There was pervasive belief that women did not need to be educated, because they would never use the knowledge they learned—most would simply become housewives.

By 1916 the Chinese had also established a school of their own, and in 1926 Kampong Kilanas had one built. All education was free, and the subjects covered were very general, including reading and writing, composition, math, geography, history, hygiene, drawing, physical education, gardening, and basketry. Soon an education inspector was appointed, and teachers were taught at the Sultan Idris Teacher Training College in Malaysia.

Bruneian students read during their religious class.

SAYING "I DO"

Getting married in Malaysia and Brunei is a colorful and important event. For one day, the bride and groom are looked on as a king and queen.

Before the wedding the parents of the bride and groom meet in order to determine the dowry, or *hantaran*, that will be given to the bride, as well as what day the wedding will take place. Sometimes the date is as much as a year in the future so there is time to complete the planning. The dowry often reaches values in the thousands of dollars and may be made up of cash, jewelry, or clothing.

The *berinai* ceremony is held before the wedding. Henna, a type of plant dye, is applied to the bride's palms and feet. This is commonly

Weddings in Brunei are elaborate and planning often starts a year before the actual ceremony.

followed by the *tukar pakaian*, during which the bride and groom put on different outfits and pose for pictures.

The *akad nikah* is a verbal contract between the father of the bride and the groom. When they both agree, a small amount of money called the *mas kahwin* is given to seal the contract. There must be three witnesses present to verify that it happened. The *kadhi*, or religious official, often lectures the groom about the importance of marriage and its many responsibilities.

After the dowry and other gifts are sent, it is time for the wedding. It is conducted by the *kadhi* in front of witnesses. Each person is asked if he or she agrees to the marriage, and then gifts are exchanged. The gifts the groom gives to his new wife are often put on display in the bridal chamber for all to see.

On the Sunday following the event people are invited to the couple's house for a feast. They eat, look at the bridal gifts, and congratulate the new couple. Each guest is promised a *bunga telur* each, otherwise known as a flower and egg. This is based on a tradition in which eggs were dyed red and placed in a cup with rice at the bottom. A paper flower was added as decoration.

The feast is informal, exciting, and loud. Guests wear bright and colorful clothing, live music plays, and when the groom first appears, he is introduced by a *hadrah* troupe, or a group of young people who bang on drums and sing religious verses. For fun some of bride's family may stop the new husband and ask him to pay an "entrance fee" before he can see his bride.

Although many Malay people still choose to hold this traditional wedding celebration, in recent years some Muslims have chosen not to do so. Their belief system deems much of the merriment as un-Islamic.

RELIGION

ISLAM IS THE PRIMARY RELIGION in Brunei, and has been for more than six centuries. It is woven into the fabric of everything people do, say, learn, wear, and eat. Elaborate mosques are found throughout the country, and the sultan's emphasis on the Melayu Islam Beraja national philosophy is evident everywhere.

More than two-thirds of the people in Brunei are Muslims, but that was not always the case. In the past, Brunei's belief system was animistic. Islam came to the land in the late 13th century. The idea was carried by the crews of merchant ships coming from India. The sultanate did a great deal of business with these merchants, and as they did so, the merchants began to share their religious beliefs. Islamic principles were discussed, and soon the sultanate had embraced this new religion. It became the reigning religion for all future generations.

Left: **Muslim men pray at a mosque in Brunei. The influence of Islam is evident in every aspect of Brunei.**

Opposite: **The Omar Ali Saifuddien mosque in Brunei.**

THE SPREAD OF ISLAM

Today, Islam is the state religion, and while the constitution does allow for freedom of religion, there are many limitations on how it can be expressed. Although people can follow other religions, these beliefs cannot be taught in any of the schools, nor can the followers of these religions talk about them in public. Photographs of religious symbols other than Islamic ones are often removed from classrooms, and all children must learn how to write in Arabic script. They must also wear Islamic dress, including the head coverings, if they attend a government

Two girls reading the Koran. All school-going children in Brunei must learn Arabic.

SULTAN OMAR ALI SAIFUDDIN'S MOSQUE

In the Bandar Seri Begawan is a mosque that is considered to be one of the most beautiful in the world. Built in 1958 for the staggering cost of $5 million, the Omar Ali Saifudden mosque is considered Brunei's masterpiece of architecture. Surrounded by an artifical lagoon with an artificial ship made of stone floating in it, the mosque features a gold dome, Italian marble walls, and Saudi Arabian carpets. It is one of the tallest buildings in the city.

school, whether or not they are actually Muslims. Now and then foreign clergy are denied entry into Brunei, and the importation of religious teaching materials is strictly controlled, along with any attempt to build a place of worship that is not Islamic. Non-Islamic groups must ask the government for permission to build or renovate churches and temples, and those structures are not allowed to display any religious symbols on the building grounds. All residents of Brunei are required to carry a card identifying their religion.

Belief in Islam affects many aspects of a person's life, because Muslims do not separate daily and religious life; they are one and the same. For example, certain things are considered haram or forbidden: drinking alcohol, eating pork or nonhalal meat, committing adultery, and touching a person of the opposite gender even casually. Even a quick handshake or clasp of the hand is not allowed. Other requirements include regular

Boys in Islamic dress on their way to school.

THE TENETS OF ISLAM

Islam is one of the world's most popular religions. It dates back to the early seventh century A.D. and started in western Arabia. A merchant named Muhammad, of Mecca, began telling of revelations he had gotten directly from Allah, or God. He believed that these were Allah's final message to the world. The prophecies that were given to Muhammad were considered to be the literal words of Allah. All 651 of the prophecies were collected into the book called the Koran, which Muslims follow closely.

The Koran states that Allah rules the world and everything and everyone in it. Because of this it is the duty of all humans to submit to Allah willingly and freely. This is why the religion is called Islam; the word means "submission." Islam states that anyone who believes in Allah will be given eternal life after death.

Followers are expected to perform the Five Pillars of Islam, or formal acts of worship. They are:

- The testimony of faith (There is no God but God, and Muhammad is His prophet)
- Mandatory prayer five times a day while facing the holy city of Mecca
- Giving of alms or money to the poor
- Fasting between dawn and dusk during the month of Ramadan
- Making a hajj, or pilgrimage, to Mecca at least once during a lifetime unless it causes financial hardship to a family.

Although women are respected in the Islamic religion, they are also required to dress modestly, obey their fathers, and avoid social contact with members of the opposite sex.

In 622 A.D. Muhammad was forced to flee from Mecca because of threats from those who did not share his beliefs. Muhammad went to Medina, from which he continued to preach his ideas and convert people. By the time he died, in 632, much of Arabia had embraced Islam.

By 750 A.D. Arabian armies had gone on to convert people throughout the Middle East and North Africa. Eventually the religion spread into Spain, East Africa, central Asia, India, and Southeast Asia.

THE PILGRIMAGE

As outlined in the Five Pillars of Islam, one of a Muslim's most important duties is to go on a pilgrimage to Mecca at least once during his or her lifetime. Mecca is in Saudi Arabia. Millions of Muslims visit the city each year, coming from places from all over the world.

Before starting out on the pilgrimage, each person enters *ihram*. This is a state of mental purity in which the person must not argue with anyone else or engage in violence. Men bathe and then put on two pieces of white cloth, while women wear a simple white dress and a head covering. The white color symbolizes "human equality and unity before God." Next, the pilgrims repeat a specific prayer called the *talbiyah*:

Here I am, O god, at Thy Command! Here I am at Thy Command!

Thou art without associate; Here I am at Thy Command! Thine are

Praise and grace and dominion! Thou art without associate.

When the pilgrim gets to Mecca's Holy Mosque, he or she enters with the right foot first and says another prayer:

In the name of Allah, may peace and blessings be upon the Messenger of Allah. Oh Allah, forgive me my sins and open To me the doors of Your mercy. I seek refuge in Allah the Almighty and in His Eminent Face and is His Eternal Dominion from the accursed Satan.

Next, the pilgrim walks in a counterclockwise procession and then performs the *sa'i*, in which he or she hurries seven times between two small hills to symbolize the search for water and food by one of Abraham's wives.

prayer and the wearing of certain clothing. The influence of Islam goes far beyond this, however. Its principles govern the country itself, as the government is run by the Sultan, or Divine Being, and his rules and laws are based on Islamic ideas.

The place of worship for Muslims is known as a mosque. Despite the fact that Islam is the most popular religion in Brunei, there are only about 100 mosques and prayer halls throughout the country. Most are only about 50 or fewer years old. This is primarily because the older mosques were made out of wood and did not last.

One of the largest mosques ever built in Brunei was during the reign of the third sultan, Sharif Ali. In the late 16th century a Spanish traveler

A Chinese temple in Brunei.

LANGUAGE

WALKING DOWN THE STREET in Brunei's capital, a person may hear two people conversing in Bahasa Melayu, a businessperson ordering lunch in English, a group of merchants chatting in Chinese, and a mother speaking to her child in Hindi or Tamil.

The main language spoken in Brunei is Malay, officially known as Bahasa Melayu. It is part of the Austronesian language family that is spoken from Madagascar through Malaysia, Indonesia, and Taiwan, all the way to Polynesia and New Zealand. Thanks to constant interaction with merchants from other lands, the Malay langugage incorporated a lot of vocabulary from other languages. There are words from Indian and Chinese languages, Arabic, Dutch, Portuguese, and English.

Although there are many languages spoken in Brunei, much of it is censored. The private press is either owned or controlled by the royal family, which will not tolerate any criticism of the government. In fact, there are laws in place that allow royalty to punish people who publish "false" or "malicious news" with prison terms of up to three years. Legislation passed in 2001 allows the government to shut down a newspaper without

Opposite: **A Bruneian school boy works on an assignment in class. Bahasa Malayu is the language of instruction in Brunei.**

COMMON WORDS AND PHRASES

Selamat pagi	Good morning
Selamat tengahari	Good afternoon
Selamat malam	Good night
Terimah kasih	Thank you
Siapa nama awak?	What is your name?
Nama saya . . .	My name is . . .
Ya	Yes
Tidak	No

having to state any cause. In addition, local radio and television broadcasts are operated and controlled by the government.

BRUNEI IN LITERATURE

Although Brunei has not produced any authors of renown, the country itself has been the setting for several books. It figures prominently in Dale Brown's novel *Armageddon*, which centers on a fictional attack on Brunei by Islamic fundamentalists with help from Malaysian forces. In Anthony Burgess's 1961 novel *Devil of a State*, he writes of an Italian father and son who are working on constructing a grand mosque in a country that is called Dunia but is actually Brunei. The mosque in the

Two muslim women reading the newspapers.

story is the sultan's palace. The story was based on Burgess's experiences working in BSB in 1958 and 1959.

The author Somerset Maugham (1874–1965) was a frequent visitor to Malaysia. Many of his short stories and novels are set there. In "Footsteps in the Jungle," he wrote about the Malaka Club, a description that hung in the clubhouse for years. He wrote,

> The club faces the sea; it is a spacious but shabby building; it has an air of neglect and when you enter you feel that you intrude. It gives you the impression that it is closed really, for alterations and repairs, and that you have taken indiscreet advantage of an open door to go where you are not wanted.

A NATION WITH POETS

In June 2007 poets from Brunei, Indonesia, and Malaysia gathered at the Indonesian Poet's Festival, held in Sumatra. It was the first time this four-day event was held, and more than 60 poets participated.

Bruneian poetry tends to be simple and direct. Writers use casual, everyday language to express their thoughts. The poet Adi Rumi wrote the following poem in honor of those lost in the Indonesian tsunami:

Brothers, your cries
are ours too.
Together we taste sadness.
We know,
you are steel-strong nation
not a flower-nation that easily droops.
Even in sorrow,
you never surrender.

The sultan's brother, His Royal Highness Mohamed Bolkiah, (*right*) with his wife. Bruneians refer to him as Penigran Perdana Wazir, stating his title, his family name, and then the name of his parents.

NAMES AND TITLES

Bruneians give several different names and titles to some people. The sultan has more than 20 names when his full title is used. These very long titles can make it difficult to know how to address a person properly. Most Bruneians are understanding when tourists or other visitors get names wrong. However, in written communication, it is essential to get a person's title completely correct. An improperly addressed letter may end up unread or thrown in the trash.

Typically, a prominent Bruneian's name will state the title first, then the family name, and finally the name of the parents. The most commonly used titles follow:

Penigran: This is a hereditary title given to relations of the royal family. The words that follow it indicate how close the person is to the sultan.

For example, Penigran Perdana Wazir: the sultan's brother, His Royal Highness Mohamed Bolkiah.

Penigran Muda: the sultan's oldest son, His Royal Highness Crown Prince.

Penigran Anak: immediate royal family as in the sultan's daughters or sisters.

Penigran: distant relatives like cousins.

Awangku: These are the distant male relatives of the royal family.

Dayangku: These are the distant female relatives of the royal family.

Pehin: Similar to a lord, this is the highest title that can be given to a commoner. It indicates a person who has led a life of excellence and service.

Dato: This is given to a person who has taken the first step toward achieving pehin status. There are many different levels, which are indicated by the names that follow the term.

Haji (male) or hajah (female): If the person has been on a pilgrimage to Mecca, he or she earns this title.

Bin (male) or binte (female): The son or daughter of someone.

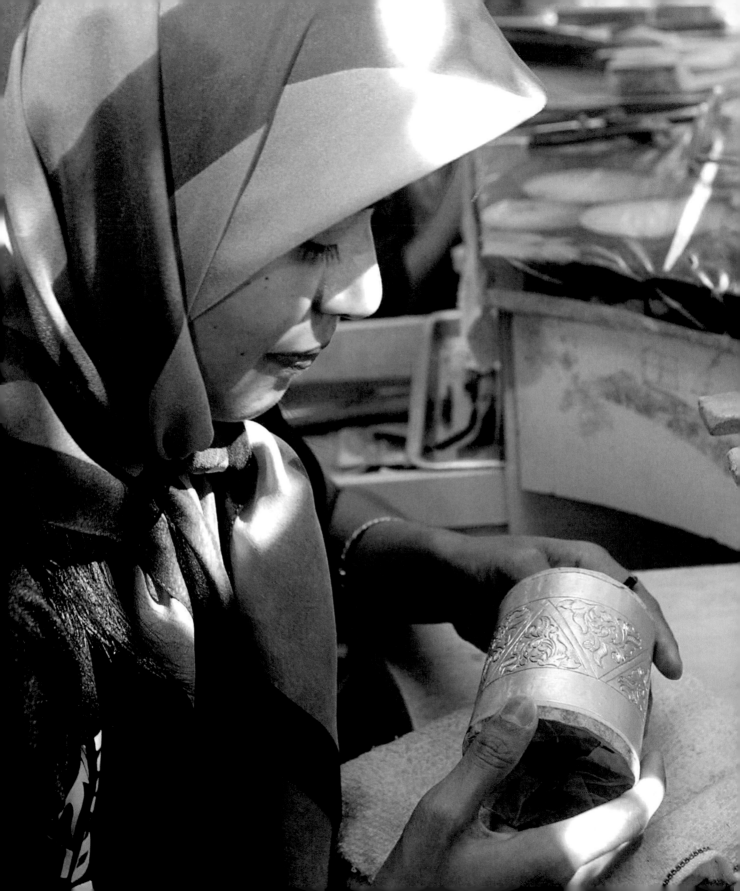

ARTS

BRUNEI HAS A RICH CULTURAL heritage that its government has worked hard to preserve. In recent years the sultan had focused on bringing back and supporting the arts and crafts popular during the nation's past. In 1975 the Arts and Handicraft Centre was opened, and it has been dedicated to restoring the skills of boatbuilding, silversmithing, bronze tooling, cloth weaving, and basket weaving. In the past the skills needed to create these handicrafts were passed down from generation to generation; now they are being passed from teacher to student.

CARVING SILVER

One of the crafts that has been brought back in recent years is silversmithing, which has a history that dates back for centuries. Legend states that the craft was practiced in Kampong Ayer and flourished until the early 16th

Left: **A silversmith delicately carves intricate patterns into silver at the Arts and Crafts Center.**

Opposite: **A student checks her engraved silverware during a course at the Arts and Handicrafts Center.**

century, with skills passing from father to son. Only a handful of craftsmen knew how to do it, and as time went by, the skill was forgotten.

In the early 1950s the government decided it wanted to start supporting Brunei's cultural arts, so it created a building in which people could display and sell their products. This became the Arts and Handicraft Centre. In 1984, thanks to its success, the program moved into a larger building.

In the past silver was obtained by melting down coins and jewelry. Today, silver sheets are imported into Brunei. The sheets are measured and then cut into the necessary shape.

An outline for an intricate design is drawn on the sheet. Often it is of plants or flowers. One of the most popular motifs is the *bunga air mulih*, a creeping, flowering vine. Other common images are *pasigupan*, or smoking pipe; *cupu*, or vase; *kiap*, or fan; *kabuk panastan*, or jar with a cover; and *tumbak*, or spear. Next, the design is filled in with hot liquid resin. Once that has hardened, an artist carefully chips it away with a small hammer and chisel until the design is clear. Silversmithers typically make ornaments, flower vases, and gongs. The largest project ever made was a pair of giant incense burners for the sultan's mosque.

WEAVING CLOTH

Like silversmithing, the skills needed for cloth weaving are passed from generation to generation. Weaving is one of Brunei's most time-honored crafts, and the country produces fabric for making beautiful gowns and sarongs. The weaving and decoration of cloth, as well as the wearing, display, and exchange of it, has been an important part of Bruneian culture for years.

The first recorded mention of cloth weaving was during Sultan Bolkiah's reign, from 1485 to 1524. The explorer Antonio Pigafetta reported seeing lovely examples of cloth. Instead of being passed from father to son, however, the skills involved were passed from mother to daughter.

As with other traditional crafts, there has been a renewed interest in cloth weaving in recent years. The women use patterns that are centuries old. One of the most famous patterns is the *jongsarat*, as it is used most often for royal and state occasions and weddings. It is used in wall coverings and in cloth meant to be given to visiting dignitaries as souvenirs.

The skill of cloth weaving was seen first in Kampung Ayer. Weaving took place inside individual homes. The women would then go outside and compare patterns and exchange tips and ideas.

Bruneian weaving does not involve any automatic machinery but a simple hand loom. Weaving gold and silver threads into the material is one element that makes this cloth special. Weaving cloth begins with

An array of thread is used for weaving cloth.

BATIK AND IKAT

There is a common saying that goes, "You are what you eat." To the people of Brunei, "You are what you wear" would be more fitting.

Two types of cloth are important to the Malay people: the batik and ikat. They are part of the culture of Brunei, Borneo, and the islands of Indonesia. While batik was considered fabric used by everyone from agricultural people to the wealthy, ikat was associated with the people living in longhouses, along the rivers and in the forests.

Batik is a dyed cotton cloth decorated through a technique known as wax-resist dyeing. Workers start with a plain piece of cotton and then carefully draw patterns with melted wax. Next, the cloth is dipped in dye. The exposed fabric soaks up the color, while the areas covered in wax do not. The wax is then boiled out of the cloth, and a new pattern is applied. Then the cloth is dipped in a different color. This continues until the pattern is complete.

In the past only certain people were allowed to wear certain batik patterns. A commoner who wore a pattern assigned to royalty, for example, was severely punished. The people who wore this type of cloth were making a cultural statement, separating themselves from the people who wore ikat and followed a more traditional lifestyle.

Ikat is made through a process similar to the one for making batik, but instead of the pattern being dyed onto finished cloth, it is created while the cloth is woven. The weaver lays out the threads to string onto her loom, precisely measuring their length. The thread is then wrapped in bark and tied up tightly so that when it is dipped in the dye, the color cannot reach all the thread. The process is repeated with different dyes.Finally, all the thread is strung on the loom. As the cloth is woven, the pattern emerges.

Ikat patterns were often specific to certain cultural groups, and patterns were passed down from generation to generation. Heirloom cloth and patterns were often exchanged as gifts during weddings.

preparing cotton thread, selecting the base color, and preparing ten bamboo spools with the specific length of thread needed for the amount of cloth being woven. This is a complex process. The weaver has to figure out exactly how many strands will be needed, usually between 1,200 and 1,500 which are then attached to the loom. Silver and gold threads are the most challenging to use, because they tangle easily.

Weaving on a loom requires hand, arm, and foot coordination. It also takes a great deal of patience and skill. Enough cloth to make an article of clothing can take ten days to more than two months to complete, depending on the intricacy of the pattern and the weaver's experience.

MAKING WEAPONS

Without a doubt, the kris is a weapon—but to the Malay people, it is much more than that. It is also a symbol of honor and ethnic identity.

Sheathed traditional Malay knives called kris.

Different styles of this knife are found throughout Malaysia and Indonesia, but each has the same basic form.

The kris has a blade between 6 and 15 inches (15 to 38 cm) long that is thin at the tip and wide at the base. Instead of being straight, the blade is wavy. It is made this way for two reasons. First, this shape will inflict a more devastating wound than will a straight blade. Second, the shape represents the lethal cobra. The knife is made with alternating layers of

THE LEGEND OF THE KRIS

No one is sure when the first kris was made, but there are many different stories about it. Here is one of the most popular.

Once upon a time, two brothers set out on a journey together. One brother had a bamboo staff, while the other had a crude blade. Both of these had come from their father, and they both possessed supernatural powers. These amazing weapons could transform into anything the brothers wished.

One day the brothers came upon a palace. They spied a beautiful girl weaving a piece of cloth on a loom. The first brother, wanting to know more about this girl, commanded his staff to turn into a bird. The other brother told his blade to change into a venomous snake. The snake snuck into the loom, bit the girl, and she fell into a deep coma.

The beautiful girl was the daughter of a king. He tried everything he could think of to revive her, but nothing worked. After several efforts, the king became desperate and announced that he would give his daughter's hand in marriage to any man who could bring her back to life.

The brother who owned the blade was the only one with an antidote, which he had gotten from his magical blade. He saved the princess, and she became his wife.

Because of this story, the blade is shaped like a snake, and its sheath represents the loom.

hard and soft steel folded repeatedly in the heat of a blacksmith's forge. At the widest part of the blade, just above the handle, the artisan often engraves a drawing of a snake's tongue or sometimes an elephant's trunk. In addition, the blade itself frequently is covered in patterns, because many makers believe that will make the weapon more effective.

In the past the men who created these weapons were considered to be more than blacksmiths; they were perceived as sorcerers. Before starting a kris, they would fast to purify themselves and then cast special spells to make their daggers more effective.

A kris handle is usually short and curved. In the past it was typically made out of ivory, but today craftspeople use wood from kulimpapa or hasana trees, because the wood is both durable and attractive.

The blade of the kris is wavy and its handle is short and curved upwards.

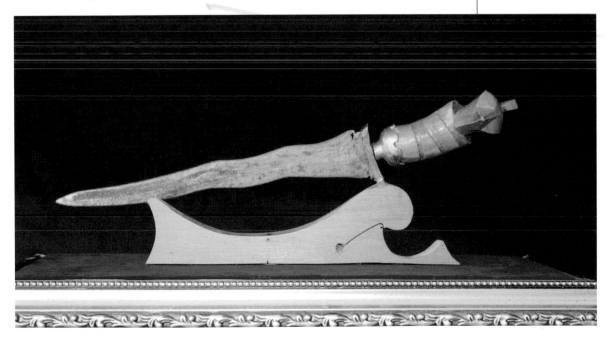

There is a lot of superstition connected to the kris. Some Malay believe that the blades obey their masters' commands and have the ability to literally fly through the air and stab a faraway enemy. Other legends state that a kris will turn on its master if he tries to use it for evil purposes. Some stories say that the dagger can make its owner invincible or warn him of approaching danger. This weapon was typically handed down from father to son and was one of the most important family heirlooms. Often, three different craftspeople were required to make a single kris: one for the blade, one for the hilt, and one for the sheath.

Thanks to the government's renewed interest in traditional Bruneian arts, kris making is viewed as an important skill that is still being taught today. For generations the process had been a closely guarded secret. Now the Arts and Handicrafts Centre shows young artisans how to heat the metal and hammer it flat. The metal is shaped, sharpened, filed, and polished. Finally, it is immersed in a bath of homemade vinegar for 24 hours. While it will not be used for hand-to-hand combat as in the past, it is important cultural symbol to be handed down in a family.

CULTURAL ART

Because Islam prohibits the depiction of living creatures, Brunei's Muslims do not create art with people or animals in it. Instead, their art focuses on foliage and abstract geometric designs. Muslim metalworkers create hammered and engraved bowls of brass or silver, while other artisans focus on creating silk cloth and carved furniture.

In Chinese art scroll painting and porcelain are important art forms. In the early 18th century some Chinese artists painted landscapes and portraits to sell overseas. Some of this art made its way to Brunei. Indian art can be seen in Hindu temples and tile work, terra-cotta sculptures, and paintings of gods and goddesses.

Some of the most vibrant art in Brunei comes from its indigenous groups. Because of the hardwoods and bamboo available in the forests, much of the art is carved from wood. The people make bowls, stools, knife handles, and other utensils, often with carved animal figures on them. Other arts include bamboo baskets and mats woven in complex, colorful patterns.

Brunei has a number of museums that demonstrate everything from relics of the past to the history of Islam to the cultural arts of the indigenous groups. The Royal Brunei Museum, which overlooks the Brunei River, is an amazing sight, especially when lit up at night. The outside is decorated with Malay designs that were inspired by the patterns found on local tombstones. The museum contains an extensive collection of Islamic art, including beautifully illustrated Korans written painstakingly in calligraphy. Other galleries feature bronzes, ceramics, and glass art. One gallery is dedicated to a shipwreck that was found off the coast several years ago. The boat sunk in the 15th century

LEISURE

BRUNEI MAY BE SMALL, but the people who live there, as well as visitors, know how to have fun. From a roller coaster-ride to a long dive, Brunei has lots of options for entertainment.

GET IN LINE, BUY A TICKET

Many visitors to Brunei plan on touring the mosques, wandering through the rain forests, and enjoying the cuisine. Going to an amusement park does not usually make it onto the list of things to do. Despite this, Brunei's capital is home to the 141-acre (57-ha) Jerudong Park Playground, an amusement park built in 1994 to honor the sultan's 48th birthday. Built at a cost of more than $1 billion, the park has an amphitheater in which celebrities such as Michael Jackson have performed.

Visitors can take rides on paddle boats, enjoying the sights of the bright Japanese carp in the waters and the lively merry-go-round which sits in the middle of the lake on an island. They can also hop aboard a replica of the American Rio Grande steam train and tour the entire park. Small children can ride on the Junior Pirate ship or Junior Sky Diver as well as the Caterpillar. Older kids enjoy the shooting gallery, bumper cars, and a ride backward in time to the age of dinosaurs on the Telecombat. Perhaps the park's favorite, however, is the Log Flume. According to the park's Web site, the ride is filled with fright and delight! "Savor the unexpected reverse drop over the edge into the unknown . . . TERROR . . . then reprieve . . . you are ok . . . you have slowed down . . . ready for another climb . . . head into the dark tunnel and before you realize that you are at the very top of the mountain . . . it's TOO LATE! Race down at great speed . . . out of control . . . SPLASH!"

Opposite: **Young boys ride their bicycles for some mid-afternoon fun.**

FESTIVALS

WHEN IT COMES TO celebrations in Brunei, it should come as little surprise that almost every event centers on either Islam or on honoring the sultan.

The first festivity of the year comes in February, on National Day. Preparations often begin two months ahead of time. The day begins with the raising of the flag. It is a time of mass prayer, as well as of colorful and exciting celebrations that commemorate achieving independence.

The next celebration, whose date varies according to the lunar calendar, is known as Ramadan. This is a holy month for Muslims. During this time

Opposite: **Dancers performing during Brunei's 20th National Day parade.**

Below: **Bruneians proudly wave their flags during Brunei's 20th National Day celebrations.**

Firecrackers can often be heard during Chinese New Year.

There is mass prayer throughout the country, and the sultan delivers a *titah* or royal address, from his palace.

Next on the calendar is the festival known as Mauludin Nabi S.A.W., which honors the Prophet Muhammad's birthday. Throughout the country Muslims read from the Koran, and the minister of religious affairs makes a speech. "It is hoped that this gathering will strengthen the vision and increase awareness of Muslims in the country, to lead a life in accordance with religion, to take heed of the teachings of Islam and follow in the steps of the Prophet Muhammad," he stated during a recent holiday.

CHINESE NEW YEAR

For the Chinese community in Brunei the most important holiday is Chinese New Year. This festival lasts for two weeks. It starts with a reunion dinner on the night of the lunar new year. This is held to encourage closer relationships between family members. For the rest of the holiday families concentrate on visiting one another, often bringing along oranges as a sign of long life and good fortune.

At these New Year celebrations people often wear red clothes and decorate with poems written on red paper. They choose red because it symbolizes fire, which, according to Chinese legend, can drive away

ANG POW

Another tradition for celebrating Chinese New Year is distributing *ang pow*, or "red packets." They are usually given to single people, teenagers, and children and contain a prize or more commonly money. The tradition dates back to the Sung Dynasty in China. Legend states that a village called Chang-Chieu was being terrorized by a giant demon that no one could defeat. Even the best warriors were vanquished. Finally, a young orphan armed with a magical sword succeeded in killing the demon. The elders of the village presented him with a red envelope filled with money to reward his courage and persistence.

The amount of money put inside an *ang pow* depends on the age of the child. The older he or she is, the more money is given. No matter how much it is, however, it is always given in even amounts, as odd numbers are a sign of loneliness and bad luck in the Chinese culture. The packets are given out not only during Chinese New Year but also at weddings and on birthdays.

Usually there is an image on the front of the envelope that wishes the recipient a long life, prosperity, and good health. Typical drawings include carp swimming among lotus flowers, fabled creatures such as dragons and phoenixes, peonies in full bloom, golden pineapples, and Buddha and children.

bad luck. Fireworks are also ignited in hopes that the crackling flames will frighten away evil spirits.

The end of Chinese New Year is marked with a lantern festival. Many of the homemade lanterns are painted with birds, animals, flowers, zodiac signs, and detailed scenes from legend and history. The lanterns are carried in nighttime parades and then hung up in temples.

Additional Chinese holidays include Qingming, or Spring Festival, in April, and the Seventh Moon Festival, in August. A colorful procession may also indicate that a wedding or funeral is taking place.

Other holidays celebrated in Brunei include Teacher's Day, Public Service Day, and Christmas. Teacher's Day is celebrated on September 23 and is held to recognize the good deeds teachers perform for the community, for religious groups, and for the country itself. The holiday is on this day to commemorate the birthday of the late sultan Haji Omar Ali Saifuddin Sa'adul Khairi Waddien, who was known for his contributions in the field of religious education. Awards are given out to teachers who have done a great job throughout the year. Many students take the opportunity to compliment their teachers and bring them small gifts. Even adults look back on their favorite teachers with fondness. "I used to dislike one particular teacher because he was strict, always lecturing me about all sorts of things," said one 43-year-old Bruneian. "But, as I grew older, his words of advice stayed with me and became my guiding light during many tough examinations, and now I impart his words to my own children."

Just a few days later, the Bruneians celebrate Public Service Day. It is held to honor Brunei's first written constitution as well as to remind government officials to always give sincere and honest public service.

FESTIVAL OF LIGHTS

For the Hindus living in Brunei, the most important festival of the year is Deepavali, a festival of lights usually celebrated in October or November. During this time, Hindu temples are decorated with paper flowers and offerings of food and clothing. Hundreds of oil lamps are lit, and most Indians purchase new clothes to wear. Tamil Indians also celebrate Thaipusam in late January or early February. Some male worshippers choose to show their religious devotion by walking through the cities with thick steel spears piercing their chests, arms, or legs. Because they are in a hypnotic trance, they do not appear to feel any pain, and their wounds rarely bleed.

Decorations like this can be seen in Hindu temples during the Festival of Lights.

FOOD

AS THE SUN GOES DOWN in Brunei's capital, farmers paddle their boats to the edge of the Kianggeh River to sell their wares. They offer bamboo tools, handmade baskets, dehydrated noodles, and *keropok*, or prawn crackers. They also offer a wide variety of fruits and vegetables. Although Bruneians know how to turn the local produce into favorite dishes, many of the vegetables and fruits would be unfamiliar to westerners.

FRUITS AND VEGETABLES

Thanks to Brunei's warm, wet weather all year round, the country is able to grow a number of unusual and exotic fruits and vegetables. Some are grown in backyard gardens and orchards. Others, such as bananas, papayas, pineapples, and watermelons, are produced on larger plantations.

One of the favorite fruits throughout Asia and especially Brunei is the durian. This fruit looks like it came from another planet. It is shaped like

Left: **Tropical fruits like bananas are readily available in Brunei all year round.**

Opposite: **Many Bruneians buy their produce from open air markets like this.**

123

A CLOSER LOOK AT THE DURIAN

In Alfred Russel Wallace's book *The Malay Archipelago*, he described his first encounter with this exotic fruit. He wrote

> The old traveller Linschott, writing in 1599, says, 'It is of such an excellent taste that it surpasses in flavour all the other fruits of the world, according to those who have tasted it.' And Doctor Paludanus adds, 'This fruit is of a hot and humid nature. To those not used to it, it seems at first to smell like rotten onions, but immediately they have tasted it they prefer it to all other food. The natives give it honourable titles, exalt it, and make verses on it.' When brought into a house the smell is often so offensive that some persons can never bear to taste it. This was my own case when I first tried it in Malacca,but in Borneo I found a ripe fruit on the ground, and, eating it out of doors, I at once became a confirmed Durian eater. . . . In fact to eat Durians is a new sensation, worth a voyage to the East to experience.

a football that is covered in sharp green spikes. When it is split open, the smell is unlike anything in the world. It reminds most people of a garlic and onion blend. Some describe it as delicious, while others call it disgusting. Inside, the fruit looks like a cross between scrambled eggs and vanilla pudding. How does it taste? It depends on who you ask.

Another unusual fruit is the egg-size rambutan. Harvested in July and August, it is also an alien-looking, oval-shaped fruit. It is no surprise that its name comes from the Malay word *rambut*, which means "hairy." The fruit is bright red and covered in long, white hairs. If a person can get past the skin, inside is sweet, juicy flesh. Fans of the rambutan caution eaters to take small bites of the fruit so as not to get any of the papery, tough skin of the seed.

The *langsat* is a type of fruit that looks like a cross between white potatoes and large grapes. They grow in clusters, and once the skin is

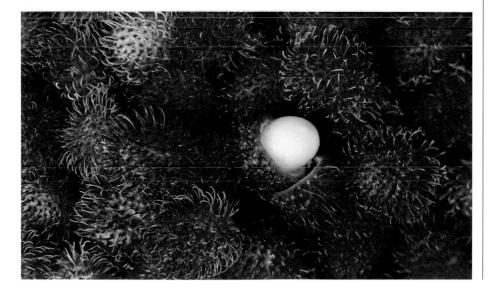

Rambutans are unusual looking fruits that boast sweet, succulent flesh.

removed, the white flesh inside tastes like a sweet grape.

The long bean is one of Brunei's most popular vegetables. Also called the cowpea, it can grow to be as long as 9 feet (2.7 m). Similar to the green beans available in this country, the pod itself is edible and is often added to Malay dishes to create a delicate crunch. Other popular Bruneian vegetables include *lamiding*, or wild tender fern shoots; rebung, or bamboo shoots; *kulat*, or fungi, and greens with names like *cangkuk manis*, *kangkung*, and *bayam*.

FAVORITE FOODS

The food eaten in Brunei is an interesting combination of Malay, Asian, Arab, Indian, and Chinese flavors. Favorite dishes include *daging masak lada hitam*, a curried beef with garlic, onion, hot chilies, and other spices; *udang sambai seral bersantan*, spicy prawns smothered in coconut milk and curry, and *serondeng padang*, chicken with coconut milk, and chilies, wrapped in leaves.

Rice and noodles are used in the majority of dishes, and coconut milk is added to everything from salads to desserts. Spicy chili peppers are often added to dishes, as is curry, a spice mixture that warms up most recipes. Meats include fish and seafood, as well as beef and chicken. According to Islamic principles, pork is forbidden. The Ministry of Religion closely monitors restaurants and confiscates any forbidden products that are found. Some families who live in rural areas also eat game birds and *sambar*, a type of barking deer.

Perhaps the favorite dish in Brunei is *ambuyat*, one that many non-Bruneians find challenging to eat. It starts with the inner stem of the sago palm tree. It is ground into a powder and then mixed with water to make a paste. This dish first became popular during World War II, when Japan took control of all the rice paddies in the country. Because the Bruneians could not access rice, they had to find something else to eat. Because *ambuyat* is bland by itself, it is served with a variety of side dishes and dipping sauces to liven it up.

Because Brunei is a Muslim country, many Islamic principles have made their way into everyday life. For example, it is considered rude to

Left: **Hot chillis being sold at a market in Brunei. Many Bruneian dishes include chilli.**

Opposite: **The long bean is added into many Bruneian dishes to give it an extra crunch.**

CHEWING ON TROUBLE

A common habit shared by people throughout much of Asia, including Brunei, is the chewing of the fruit from the betel palm. This spicy, datelike fruit gives the chewer a slight jolt of energy, similar to the effect of drinking several cups of coffee. In 2003 the World Health Organization conducted a study that showed betel nuts can cause oral cancer. Unfortunately, that has not stopped many people from chewing it. People still chew it for a number of reasons, including freshening the breath, fighting off hunger, using it as a substitute for cigarettes, or obtaining a high.

Nasi goreng, or fried rice, is sometimes also served with an egg.

use your left hand to eat or shake hands, as Muslims consider the left hand to be unclean. In addition, Muslims are not allowed, by religious law, to eat food that is derived from any form of pork. The meat that is allowed must be from animals that have been killed according to strict religious regulations. The term for this acceptable meat is halal.

THE CHINESE AND INDIAN INFLUENCES

The Chinese influence on Bruneian food can be tasted in such common dishes as *nasi goreng*, fried rice, and *mee goreng*, fried noodles. Egg rolls, or *lumpia*, are popular, as are dim sum appetizers and a clear fish soup containing thin noodles.

Indian cuisine influences local cuisine as well. It includes open-air food stalls serving *roti canai*, thin pancakes dipped in curry sauce, or *murtabak*, pancakes stuffed with lamb and onion curry.

The food of Brunei is a reflection of the people who live in the country. Like the Bruneians themselves, the combination makes for exotic flavors and exciting meals.

SWEET RICE AND BEANS

1 pound rice
⅓ cup dried green beans
4 cloves
1 teaspoon cardamom powder
1 teaspoon butter
5 cups milk
2 tablespoons raisins
3 ounces cashews
½ pound brown sugar

Dry-fry the beans until roasted. In a heavy pan combine rice, beans, cloves, cardamom, butter, and milk. Cook over low heat until the rice and beans are soft and the milk is absorbed. Remove pan from heat. Heat and fry raisins and cashews until browned. Add to the rice and beans. Put pan on low heat. Gradually add the brown sugar, stirring until dissolved. Cook until the mixture thickens. Remove from heat. Cool and serve.

SPICED ROAST CHICKEN

1½ tablespoons fresh lime juice
1 tablespoon brown sugar
¼ teaspoon cayenne pepper
¼ teaspoon ground clove
½ teaspoon ground cinnamon
½ teaspoon ground ginger
1 teaspoon black pepper
½ teaspoon salt
½ teaspoon dried thyme leaves
1 three-pound whole chicken
1 tablespoon vegetable oil

Preheat oven to 325 °F (165 °C). In a small bowl, combine the lime juice and brown sugar; set aside. Mix together the cayenne pepper, cloves, cinnamon, ginger, pepper, salt, and thyme leaves. Brush the chicken with oil, then coat it with the spice mixture. Place in a roasting pan, and bake about 90 minutes, or until the juices run clear or a meat thermometer inserted in thickest part of the thigh reaches 180 °F (82 °C). Baste the chicken with the sauce every 20 minutes while it is cooking. Allow the chicken to rest for 10 minutes before carving.

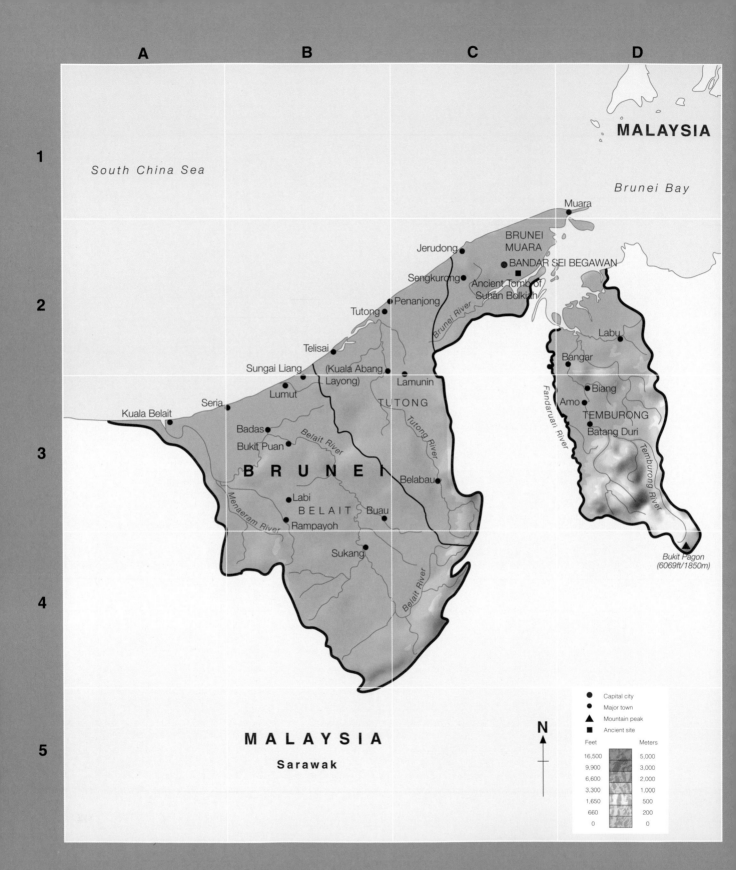

A B C D

1

South China Sea

MALAYSIA

Brunei Bay

Muara

BRUNEI
MUARA

Jerudong

BANDAR SEI BEGAWAN

Sengkurong

Ancient Tomb of
Sultan Bolkiah

Penanjong

Tutong

Brunei River

Labu

Telisai

Bangar

Sungai Liang

(Kuala Abang
Layong)

Lamunin

Biang

Seria

Lumut

TUTONG

Amo

TEMBURONG

Kuala Belait

Batang Duri

Badas

Belait River

Tutong River

Bukit Puan

Fandaruan River

Tenburong River

B R U N E I

Belabau

Labi

BELAIT

Buau

Menaeram River

Rampayoh

Bukit Pagon
(6069ft/1850m)

Sukang

Belait River

2

3

4

5

MALAYSIA

Sarawak

N

● Capital city
• Major town
▲ Mountain peak
■ Ancient site

Feet   Meters

16,500   5,000
9,900   3,000
6,600   2,000
3,300   1,000
1,650   500
660   200
0   0

MAP OF BRUNEI

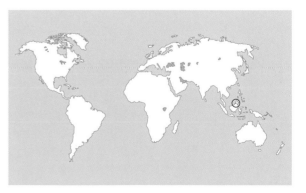

ECONOMIC BRUNEI

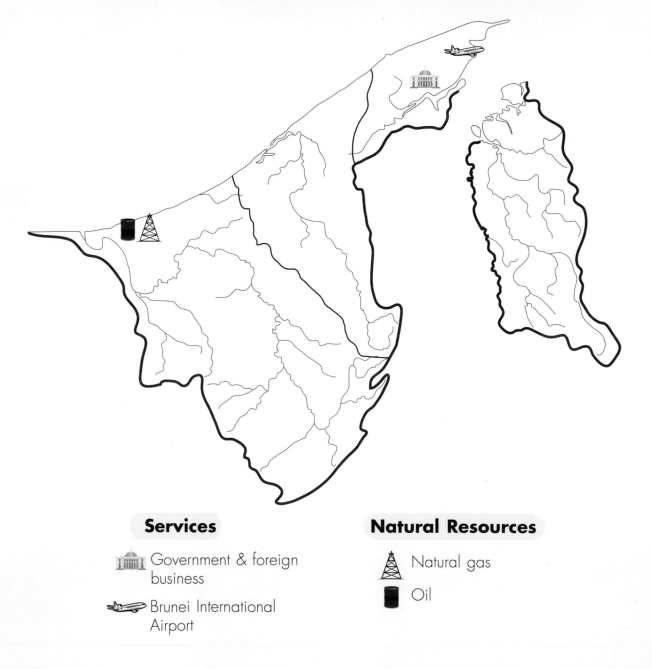

Services

🏛 Government & foreign business

✈ Brunei International Airport

Natural Resources

⛏ Natural gas

🛢 Oil

ABOUT THE ECONOMY

OVERVIEW
Primarily dependent on the export of petroleum products; there is growing interest and response in tourism and agriculture.

GROSS DOMESTIC PRODUCT (GDP)
$25,600 per capita (est. 2005)

IMPORTS
$1.481 billion

EXPORTS
$6.247 billion

INFLATION RATE
1.1 percent

UNEMPLOYMENT RATE
4 percent

TRADE PARTNERS
Japan, Indonesia, South Korea, Australia, Singapore, Malaysia, United Kingdom, Japan, China, Thailand, South Korea

CURRENCY
Bruneian dollar
USD 1 = BND 1.444 (2008)

AGRICULTURAL PRODUCTS
rice, vegetables, fruit, chickens, water buffalo, cattle, goats, eggs

INDUSTRIAL PRODUCTS
petroleum, petroleum refining, liquefied natural gas, construction

CULTURAL BRUNEI

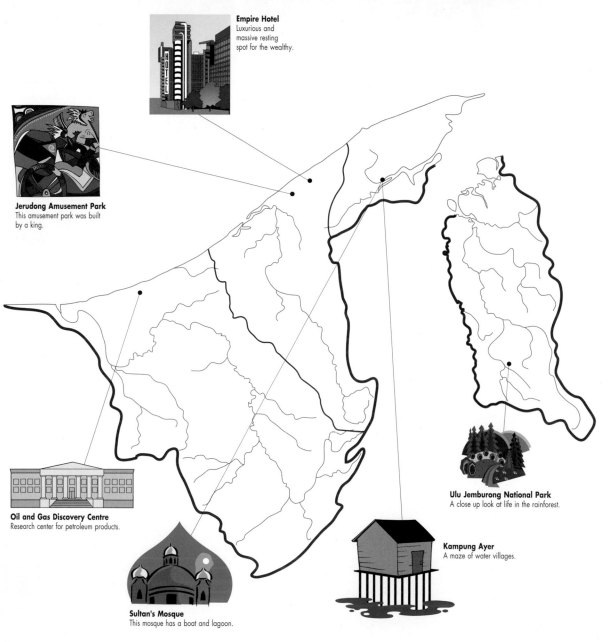

Empire Hotel
Luxurious and massive resting spot for the wealthy.

Jerudong Amusement Park
This amusement park was built by a king.

Oil and Gas Discovery Centre
Research center for petroleum products.

Sultan's Mosque
This mosque has a boat and lagoon.

Ulu Jemburong National Park
A close up look at life in the rainforest.

Kampung Ayer
A maze of water villages.

ABOUT THE CULTURE

HOLIDAYS AND FESTIVALS
Ramadan; Hari Raya Aidilfitri; Hari Raya Korban; Prophet's birthday; Teacher's Day; Public Service Day; Chinese New Year; Springfest; Seventh Moon Festival; Deepavali

OFFICIAL NAME
Negara Brunei Darussalam

COUNTRY FLAG
yellow background with two black and white diagonal stripes, with a red national emblem in the center

NATIONAL ANTHEM
"Alla Peliharakan Sultan" or "God Bless His Highness with a Long Life"

MAJOR CITIES
Districts: Belait, Temburong, Tutong, Brunei-Muara

ETHNIC GROUPS
Malay, Chinese, Indigenous, Other

RELIGION
Islam

LIFE EXPECTANCY
74.4 male; 77.4 female

LITERACY RATE
93.7 percent

TIME LINE

IN BRUNEI	IN THE WORLD

2500 B.C.
Senoi people come to the area.

1500–500 B.C.
Proto-Malay people come to the area.

7th century
Entrepôts develop.

1079–1082
Capital of the Srivijaya Empire moves from Palembang to Melayu.

323 B.C.
Alexander the Great's empire stretches from Greece to India.

1000
The Chinese perfect gunpowder and begin to use it in warfare.

1100
Rise of the Incan Civilization in Peru.

1206–1368
Genghis Khan unifies the Mongols and starts conquest of the world. At its height, the Mongol Empire under Kublai Khan stretches from China to Persia and parts of Europe and Russia.

1275
Majapahit Empire from Java invades Srivijaya Empire.

1405
Agreement is made between Melaka and Chinese emperor; Islam is accepted by sultan.

1511
The Portuguese attack and capture Melaka.

1521
Pigafetta visits Brunei with Magellan.

1529
The Treaty of Zaragossa is signed.

End of 16th century
The Dutch come to Johor.

1641
The Dutch take Melaka.

1558–1603
Reign of Elizabeth I of England

1776
U.S. Declaration of Independence

1789–99
The French Revolution

1839
James Brooke comes from England; era of White Rajahs begins.

1861
The U.S. Civil War begins.

1869
The Suez Canal is opened.

1888
Brunei becomes a British protectorate.

1899
The first oil well is dug in Brunei.

1912
The first school in Brunei is opened.

1914
World War I begins.

IN BRUNEI	IN THE WORLD

IN BRUNEI

1929
Major oil deposits are discovered in Brunei.
1938
Excavations begin in Ulu Perak.
1941–1945
World War II takes place; the Japanese invade Brunei.
1953
Brunei declares itself a welfare state.

1958
Skull found in Niah Cave; sultan's palace is built.
1959
First constitution is written.
1963
Brunei decides to remain independent of the Federation of Malaysia.
1967
Sultan Omar Ali Saifuddin abdicates, the current sultan, Bolkiah, takes his place.
1971
The constitution is amended.
1984
Brunei becomes independent of Britain.
1990
The Malay Muslim Monarchy philosophy is introduced.
1992
The study of Islam is required in all schools.
1997
Prince Jefri is relieved of his ministerial post.

2004
The sultan agrees to reopen Parliament.
2007
Brunei joins the Heart of Borneo program.

IN THE WORLD

1939
World War II begins.
1941
Japan attacks Pearl Harbor.
1945
The United States drops atomic bombs on Hiroshima and Nagasaki.
1949
The North Atlantic Treaty Organization (NATO) is formed.

1966–69
The Chinese Cultural Revolution.

1986
Nuclear power disaster at Chernobyl in Ukraine

1991
Breakup of the Soviet Union.

1997
Hong Kong is returned to China.
2001
Terrorists crash planes in New York, Washington D.C., and Pennsylvania.
2003
War in Iraq begins.

GLOSSARY

animism
The belief that natural objects, natural phenomena, and the universe itself possess souls.

annex
To incorporate (territory) into the domain of a city, country, or state.

calligraphy
Fancy penmanship, especially highly decorative handwriting, as with a great many flourishes.

camphor
A whitish, translucent, crystalline, pleasant-odored substance obtained from the camphor tree, used chiefly in the manufacture of celluloid and in medicine as a counter-irritant for infections and in the treatment of pain and itching.

carnivorous
Flesh eating.

ecotourists
Trravelers who visit places that are environmentally attractive and/or educational.

edible
Fit to be eaten.

excavation
An area in which digging has been done or is in progress, as an archaeological site.

expatriate
To withdraw (oneself) from residence in one's native country.

falsetto
An unnaturally or artificially high pitched voice or register.

malicious
Full of, characterized by, or showing malice; malevolent; spiteful.

marionette
A puppet manipulated from above by strings attached to its jointed limbs.

protectorate
A state or territory that is controlled and protected by another.

reincarnation
The belief that the soul, on death of the body, comes back to earth in another body or form.

resin
Sticky substance provided by trees.

FURTHER INFORMATION

WEBSITES

CIA Factbook: Brunei. www.cia.gov/library/publications/the-world-factbook/geos/bx.html
Country Profile at BBC. http://news.bbc.co.uk/2/hi/asia-pacific/country_profiles/1298607.stm
The government of Brunei. www.brunei.gov.bn/
U.S. Department of State. www.state.gov/r/pa/ei/bgn/2700.htm
World Guide at Lonely Planet. www.lonelyplanet.com/worldguide/destinations/asia/brunei

ORGANIZATIONS

Brunei Tourism
Jalan Menteri Besar
Bandar Seri Begawan BB3910
Brunei Darussalam
www.tourismbrunei.com

High Commission of Brunei Darussalam in the UK
19-20 Belgrave Square
London SW1X 8PG United Kingdom

Embassy of Brunei Darussalam in the USA
3520 International Court, NW
Washington, DC 20008
www.bruneiembassy.org

BIBLIOGRAPHY

Major, John S. *The Land and People of Malaysia and Brunei.* New York: Harpercollins, 1965.

Rough Guides. *The Rough Guide to Malaysia, Singapore and Brunei.* New York: Rough Guide Publishing, 2006.

Richmond, Simon, et al. *Malaysia, Singapore and Brunei.* Oakland, CA: Lonely Planet Publications, 2007.

AsiaRecipe.com: Brunei: http://asiarecipe.com/bruculture.html

BBC Country Profile: Brunei: http://news.bbc.co.uk/2/hi/asia-pacific/country_profiles/1298607.stm

BBC Timelin: Brunei: http://news.bbc.co.uk/2/hi/asia-pacific/country_profiles/1298648.stm

Brunei: The Abode of Peace: www.jadeddragon.com/articles/brunei03.html

Countries and Their Cultures: Culture of Brunei Darussalem: www.everyculture.com/Bo-co/Brunei-Darussalam.html

Drying Up?: www.iht.com/articles/2000/03/24/brunei.2.t.php

Ecology Asia: Brunei Bag: www.ecologyasia.com/html-loc/brunei-bay.htm

Encyclopedia Britannic: Brunei Plant and Animal Life: www.britannica.com/eb/article-52436/Brunei

Encyclopedia of the Nations: Brunei Darussalem: www.nationsencyclopedia.com/Asia-and-Oceania/Brunei-Darussalam.html

Freedom House: www.freedomhouse.org

International Herald Tribune: Lavish Spending/Economic Warning Signs: Is Brunei's Well of Prosperity

Saudi Arabian Airlines: Sniffing Out the Proboseis Monkey on Brunei's Damuan River: http://pr.sv.net/aw/2006/July2006/english/pages037.htm

The Government of Brunei: National Philosophy: www.brunei.gov.bn/government/mib.htm

Travellers Worldwide: About Brunei Darussalam: www.travellersworldwide.com/14-brunei/14-brunei-about.htm

U.S. Department of State Background Nok: Brunei Darussalem: www.state.gov/r/pa/ei/bgn/2700.htm

Wedding Customs of "Puak Tutong": www.freewebs.com/hfakhriah/engagement.htm

Wedding Customs Around the Muslim World: The Malay Wedding: www.zawaj.com/weddingways/malay.html

World Religions: Islam: www.religioustolerance.org/islam.htm

INDEX